EAST ANGLIA

Its Tideways and Byways

EAST ANGLIA
Its Tideways and Byways

GEOFFREY MORGAN

Illustrated by
Robin Sterndale Bennett

ROBERT HALE · LONDON

Set in Sabon by Derek Doyle & Associates, Mold, Clwyd.
Printed in Great Britain by
St Edmundsbury Press Ltd, Bury St Edmunds, Suffolk.
Bound by WBC Bookbinders Ltd, Bridgend, Glamorgan.

Contents

	Acknowledgements	7
	Map	10
	Introduction	11
1	The Backwaters	17
2	Constable's River	37
3	The Commercial Tideway	68
4	The Deben Shores	86
5	The Magic of the Estuaries	106
6	Reeds and Saltings	130
7	The Broadland Waterways	144
8	The North Norfolk Inlets	165
9	The Wash to Denver	180
	Glossary	193
	Useful Addresses	195
	Bibliography	199
	Index	201

Books by Geoffrey Morgan

FICTION
Lame Duck
The Small Wish
Tea with Mr Timothy
A Small Piece of Paradise
A Touch of Magic
A Window of Sky
The View from Prospect
Summer of the Seals
Flip: The Story of a Seal
The White Dolphin

NON-FICTION
Soldier Bear (with W.A. Lasocki)

Acknowledgements

One of the rewards of researching this book – apart from going back to familiar places and exploring some that are not so familiar – has been to meet so many helpful people, all of whom have given their co-operation so freely.

I should like to thank all those to whom I have referred in the text – harbour masters, Trinity House officers, officials of the national and county trusts and other conservation organizations, and especially the wardens who gave me so much of their time afloat and ashore: Frank Bloom of the Walton Backwaters; Lieutenant-Colonel Hawkes of Skippers Island; John Partridge, RSPB warden of Havergate Island; and National Trust wardens at Blakeney and Brancaster Joe Reed and Richard Lowe. I should also like to include here John Perryman of the Norfolk Wherry Trust, Charles Underwood of Orford and Winifred Cooper of the Harwich Society.

I am most grateful to Dr Sue Mayer of the RSPCA Seal Unit at Docking and to Sheila Anderson of the Sea Mammal Research Unit for their specialist assistance, and to John Watkins of Gedney Dyke, Lincolnshire, and the late Bill Vaughan of the SMRU, who for many years have contributed to my knowledge of seals in the Wash and who first introduced me to the marshes and sands of this fascinating and remote area.

I am also grateful to Maurice Griffiths for permisison to include the evocative extract from his book *The Magic of the Swatchways*, and to the publishers of those books from which I have quoted.

It would have been impossible to cover most of the tidal creeks and waterways in the various regions I have included without the aid of boats available in the appropriate geographical locations, and amongst the many friends who gave their time and their craft in furthering my research I am indebted to Cy Blackwell, Phil Cole, Bob Horne, Jerry Pocock, Ron Hunting, John Buckley and Len Allen.

For his practical help and advice on a number of aspects I should like to thank Bob Malster; my appreciation is also due to Robin Sterndale Bennett, who tramped and boated with me through so much of the region in varying weather conditions without complaint.

Finally, I should emphasize that where I have referred to private property the owner's privacy should be respected.

To
Ann
for her supportive role throughout

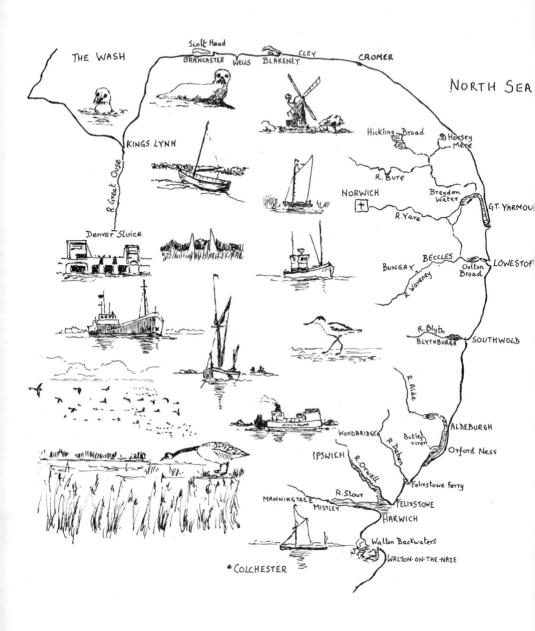

THE WASH

Scolt Head
BRANCASTER   WELLS   BLAKENEY   CLEY   CROMER

NORTH SEA

KINGS LYNN

Hickling Broad   Horsey Mere

R. Great Ouse

R. Bure

NORWICH   Breydon Water   GT. YARMOUTH

R. Yare

Denver Sluice

BECCLES

BUNGAY   Oulton Broad   LOWESTOFT

R. Waveney

R. Blyth
BLYTHBURGH   SOUTHWOLD

R. Alde

ALDEBURGH

WOODBRIDGE   Butley river

IPSWICH   R. Deben   Orford Ness

R. Orwell   Felixstowe Ferry

MANNINGTREE   R. Stour
MISTLEY   FELIXSTOWE

HARWICH

Walton Backwaters

WALTON·ON·THE·NAZE

COLCHESTER

Introduction

The tideways of East Anglia, with their mudflats, marshes and reeds and the country rising from them, have fascinated me since the early 1930s. Boyhood summers on the Stour estuary, the river dividing the counties of Essex and Suffolk, where my brother and I taught ourselves to sail, were a never-to-be-repeated introduction to the region, for at that time the area remained almost untouched by development.

The motor car was still a fairly scarce commodity, particularly in the country, so there was little traffic on the winding lanes, and on the river – well, apart from a weekend cruising yacht, an occasional fishing-boat and at intervals the appearance of the whalers manned by the boys of HMS *Ganges*, the naval training establishment at Shotley, the only regular traffic on the river was the sailing-barge.

There were some 700 of these old sailing-craft trading before the war, their black or grey hulls under an enormous spread of red-ochred canvas, manned by a skipper and his mate, plying the Thames estuary and the east-coast ports with a variety of cargoes, from hay and corn to shingle and timber. They were a lovely sight – and still are, for although they no longer trade, some fifty or more remain, restored and sailed by private owners and trusts as well as some of the companies which ran fleets during the working life of these craft. They can still be seen in fleets, in competition for cups not cargoes, at the annual barge matches in June, perhaps the best-known event being the Pin Mill match organized by the Pin Mill Sailing Club on the Orwell river.

If the sailing-barges in the late thirties were beginning to give way to diesel-driven vessels, it was not immediately apparent on the Stour; their unique spritsail rig was still a familiar sight, and the rattle of their anchor chains could still be heard ashore as they anchored in the channel for the night or waited for the tide to take them up to the maltings at Mistley. It was not an unusual event between tides to find one on Wrabness hard for a quick coat of tar below the waterline. We came to know some of the sailormen and once enjoyed a leisurely passage down to Harwich, to sail back in our dinghy with the tide.

After the bustle of Harwich the river above Erwarton Ness, on the Suffolk side, seemed a peaceful backwater, although Harwich at that time could be described as a quiet haven compared with what it is today. The old port still had an atmosphere of the great days of sail, with its scents of tar, rope and timber. Barges had been built there from before the turn of the century, and there was still a yard where they were repaired, just north of the town pier, which is now a modern dock terminal. A Trinity House depot was there, the Hook of Holland ferry used Parkeston Quay; there were the *Ganges* whalers, the Harwich shrimp boats, the small ferries serving Shotley and Felixstowe, some shipping from Ipswich and during the sailing season some cruising-yachts and racing-boats.

Across the harbour on the Felixstowe side were the crane and hangars of the flying-boat base, and almost within a stone's throw of these the little dock where the Harwich–Felixstowe ferry berthed. Small warehouses lined this basin on one side; on the other were the maltings and, just beyond, a low cluster of storage tanks. Landing there from a yacht, you would never find more than a barge or two alongside and perhaps a small coaster.

How different it is now! The flying-boat station has long since gone, and the dock, although still there, is almost swallowed up in the great expanse of the international port which is still expanding. But even in those days and just after the war the harbour traffic was light enough to allow the huge Sunderland flying-boats to run their taxi-ing tests, and sailing a small boat in the vicinity when these craft were droning across in a skirt of spray could cause some apprehensive moments to a young helmsman.

But up river we sailed into solitude, creeping over the vast mudflats with a rising tide to nose the dinghy onto some sandy shore and picnic under a wooded bank. We felt we had landed on a desert island.

Things were slow to change after the war. In the eyes of the outsider, East Anglia remained a flat, sprawling chunk of land reaching into the North Sea, leading nowhere and fanned by a cold east wind that was said to come from Siberia; the common view of the casual visitor was of a bleak country of farmland, heathland, pine forests, waterways, marshes, saltings and mud. Apart from a few holiday-makers who sailed the Broads or enjoyed the reserved atmosphere of the small coastal towns, or the naturalist who tramped the marshes or the dike walls, the region, for the most part, remained cocooned in its agriculture and ancient history.

In the last decade or two, the scene has changed dramatically, particularly in the south of the region. If the process was slow, gradual in the beginning, the transformation has been rapid in the past few years. Commerce and light industry, the leisure and tourist industries have opened up the area; the development of communications, the modernization of the railways and the roads and the increasing affluence, combined with more leisure time, have enabled more and more people to take advantage of the opportunities and facilities provided. East Anglia has certainly lost its insular image.

All this has had its effect on the old east-coast harbours and the tidal rivers that serve them. Most of the smaller ports that were once busy with sailing-traders now cater for the yachtsman, and this is emphasized especially in the south by the weekend and holiday scene – the leisure-fleets under sail and power that go down to the sea.

The maritime trade, too, has expanded rapidly, most noticeably at Harwich, Felixstowe and Ipswich. The decline of commercial traffic at Southampton and on the London river speeded the changes that arrived with the container ship and the roll-on/roll-off (ro-ro) ferry, and from such a small beginning Felixstowe has rapidly developed into one of the most successful ports in the UK, serving most of the trading nations of the world. Harwich and Parkeston, too, with their North Sea ro-ro ferries, have increased their capacity; add to all this development the expansion of Ipswich docks and the pleasure craft from the old mooring trots and the new marinas, and you will find the Orwell estuary and Harwich harbour very busy places indeed.

As a consequence, Felixstowe itself has expanded, particularly with much new development behind the port, although this has not detracted from its popularity as a holiday resort; in fact, the Orwell Bridge and the modern A45, which takes the container traffic, have provided easier access to the town for the holiday motorist and the day-tripper.

Moving up the coast, the scene has not changed so dramatically except for the blot at Sizewell, where the second nuclear power station is building – and this on the 'Heritage Coast!'

Apart from Lowestoft and Great Yarmouth, which have always been busy ports as well as holiday venues and latterly have catered for the North Sea gas industry, the coastal towns and villages have mostly retained the physical shape and reserved atmosphere that have always been their attraction. One major incursion north along the coast is the gas terminal at Bacton; otherwise little has changed: the seaside towns of Sheringham and Cromer cling to their conservative characters midst the growing holiday traffic, whilst the villages and tidal inlets along the north Norfolk coast, with their bird reserves and inshore fishing, sand-dunes and marshes, have always held for me a wild and timeless solitude that no tourist attraction can eclipse.

This coastal scenery makes a dramatic change with the cliffs at Hunstanton, a holiday town overlooking the Wash, that great expanse of sandbanks and sea where the common seal live and breed in one of Britain's largest colonies. From here south the coastline reverts mainly to the physical features of the north, but without the tidal inlets, until you reach the mouth of the Great Ouse and the ancient port of King's Lynn.

For obvious reasons, the most marked changes in East Anglia are in the south. Despite the residential and industrial expansion, plus the tourist traffic and the services that cater for them, so much of the beauty of the countryside remains to be seen and enjoyed – the gentle valleys, the fine churches, the great houses, the wool villages, the market towns; their splendour has been illustrated by numerous artists, their history recorded by many writers. That so much of the scene remains unspoiled in a time of rapid change is due largely to the vigilance of the conservation bodies, trusts and associations that play such an active role in preserving East Anglia's heritage and wildlife.

As for the scenery – well, provided your taste is not for mountains and waterfalls, there are few regions that offer such a wealth of contrasts: lush water-meadows, wooded slopes rising from shallow valleys, deserted beaches, reed-fringed waterways, dunes and marshes and muddy estuaries, and from so many points of view always the wide-open skies.

Such scenery inspired some of England's best painters. Two of the most famous were East Anglians: Gainsborough, who was born in Sudbury and who, although perhaps best-known for his portraits of beautiful women in picture-hats, used the pastoral backgrounds of his native locality in many of his family portrayals; Constable, born in East Bergholt, whose landscapes in and around the Stour Valley have given his name to this lush part of the country. The scenes are still there, as many East Anglian artists of today illustrate so successfully.

It goes without saying that modern communications have scarred some of the scenery, although in many instances they have fortunately been of minimal intrusion. The A12 that crosses the Stour Valley at Stratford St Mary has not greatly changed the river valley above and below it; much of it is as Constable saw it two centuries ago when he wrote: 'The beauty of the surrounding scenery, its gentle declivities, its luxuriant meadow flats sprinkled with flocks and herds, its well-cultivated uplands, its woods and rivers, with numerous scattered villages and churches, farms and picturesque cottages, all impart to this particular spot an amenity and elegance hardly anywhere else to be found.'

These scenes and so many others of the same quality can be found all over East Anglia. Many of them border the tidal rivers, creeks and inlets and make up the valleys and the villages and harbour the wildlife habitats, all pervaded with that intangible atmosphere that heralds the nearness of the sea.

Robin and I have attempted to portray some of these places, seeking out their locations by road, by water and on foot. Tidal water there is in plenty, but it is not our intention here to provide a navigating aid for the sailor; there are several publications available on the subject for the yachtsman, one of the best and most comprehensive being *East Coast Rivers* by Jack H. Cootes, regularly brought up to date. If the sailor has the time and the inclination to take the dinghy from many of the attractive anchorages and stretch his (or her) legs ashore, we are confident he (or she) will find the reward worthwhile.

If the insular image of East Anglia has changed, the diverse scenic charm of the countryside and coast, the beauty of its medieval and Gothic architecture, have not. All these and many more remain to be enjoyed; we hope our reflections on some of them will help the visitor, the new resident and – dare we say? – the native to enjoy them even more.

Opinions differ on the definition of the boundary of East Anglia, particularly in the south. Some will draw a line across mid-Essex, others go north or even south of it. Although we have taken the historical view that the southern frontier did not go south of the Stour, we have included the border area on the Essex side, together with that tidal inlet just south of Harwich that opens onto a maze of channels, drying creeks, mudflats and islands, which comprises the Walton Backwaters.

G.M.

---------- 1 ----------

The Backwaters

'There – coming over now ... the first arrivals.' The small skein of brent-geese appeared ahead of us, then wheeled high over the creek and glided down to the shallows fringing the saltings of Horsey Island. Frank Bloom, warden of the Walton Backwaters, slowed the launch, turned across the channel and cut the engine, and we drifted slowly towards the marshy inlet where the geese had settled. As the black-headed arrivals, no larger than mallard ducks, swam towards the head of the narrow waterway, we counted them. Forty-six. A small spearhead of the many hundreds that would be arriving from the far north before winter.

It was the first day of October. The sky was a deep blue, a great arc that lay back the horizon across marsh and water as far as the eye could see. The placid surface of the Wade dazzled us with reflected sunlight. It was as warm as late summer; crystal clear – a typical East Anglian autumn day under a typical East Anglian sky.

We were nearing the end of our patrol. Looking back on our wake, we could see a maze of waterways, separating substantial islands with sea-walls, and islets that vanished under a rising tide, marshy expanses terminating in gently sloping banks of mud where wading birds fed; prominent channels – Hamford Water, Walton Channel, opening out from the entrance at the southern end of Dovercourt Bay; Oakley Creek winding up between Bramble and Peewit Islands; Landermere and Beaumont Creeks at the south-western end of Hamford Water, taking us as far as the depth would allow; the oyster-layings on the bed of Kirby Creek, the scent of the saltings flanking Skippers Island, the shallow,

Part of Walton Backwaters

mere-like expanse of the Wade, where we had counted the brent, and ahead, our berth in the Twizzle. And for most of the day our only company – sea birds, duck and a variety of waders and, as a bonus, a brief glimpse of the seals.

Six common seals are in residence here; a pair of them surfaced to investigate us, round, dog-like heads and large, luminous eyes watching us with characteristic curiosity. I had seen some of them in the past hauled out on the Pye Sand just outside the entrance, and it was particularly reassuring to see them on this occasion and to find them free of the disease which had so tragically decimated the large colonies on the Norfolk coast and in the Wash during the summer and autumn of 1988.

I had sailed into the Backwaters on many occasions, but they had served only as a brief port of call with a companion or two who wanted to be under way again to somewhere else. There never seemed to be the time or the opportunity to sit the yacht in the shallows and take the dinghy to the remote places at the tidal limits, so for the most part I was acquainted with only the most popular anchorages – Hamford Water, Walton Channel and, latterly, the marina. But from my boat patrols with Frank Bloom and my observations from the land on sea-wall and creekside hikes, I derived for the first time a complete picture of the whole area; a picture that has changed little from my very first introduction in the early 1930s, which was not physical but through the pen of Maurice Griffiths, whose evocative book of pre-war sailing days, *The Magic of The Swatchways*, first appeared in 1932.

The Backwaters were a favourite haunt of Maurice Griffiths in those days, particularly when he sought absolute solitude to write, and on those occasions he would sail alone in his little barge yacht *Swan*, seeking an anchorage before nightfall close to the head of one of the creeks and there, as the tide ebbed away, leaving his yacht to settle upright on the mud (just like her big sister the sailing-barge), the oncoming night would cocoon man and boat in complete isolation.

Of the many single-handed experiences he had in a number of different yachts, the one he records in his book when he sailed *Swan* into the autumn dusk towards the head of Landermere and Beaumont creeks depicted for me the fascination of this unique area of land and water. The essence of it may be summed up in one or two extracts of the many I could quote:

As quickly as it had narrowed the creek opened out again, and revealed before me a dim expanse of water on which ripples chased one another amongst tall grass that appeared here and there above the placid surface. It was now too dark to see the quay at the head of the creek, but one or two lights told where the cottages that looked over the water at high tide stood near the wharf. There is a faint channel that leads right up to Beaumont Quay, but I did not know it, and although I saw one stray withy apparently out in the middle I knew not which side of it the deeper water lay ...

Then she stopped. It was no use trying to get any nearer to the quay [Landermere] now. She was aground for the night ...

It was dark now ... A train was pulling out of Frinton station. A dog heard it and barked. A curlew from somewhere over Skippers Island called his mate ... Voices were coming faintly from the direction of the quay, and a motor horn broke the stillness of the Kirby road. And the mud all round was hissing as the last of the tide receded from sight, leaving a thin tortuous rivulet that trickled down the middle of the creek a few feet from the yacht's bow.

The night grew colder ... and above the uncertain marshes through which we had threaded our way a mist was rising, ghostlike, unfolding its white coils over the damp grass and making the scene vague ... mysterious ...

Off Landermere

It was eerie and lonely out here, and somehow every sound ceased, as though the rest of the world had suddenly been cut off ... A dead, uncanny silence reigned over everything. And now the mist was around us, blotting out everything but the dark mass of the dinghy resting on the mud and the four yellow beams of light that escaped through the [cabin] portlights ...

But what a change next morning! The early sun was glinting on the dew-covered deck, and what had been the previous night murky stretches of uncertain mud was now an expanse of mirror-like water. Hardly a breath stirred, and the reflections of the trees were reproduced faithfully on the placid surface. From the wharf a barge was drifting down, light, her familiar topsail and big mainsail set in the hope of catching any draught that was going. It was just high water, and the islands that had last night appeared as high banks of mud with gaunt sedge on top, now seemed to be flat fields of coarse grass out of which grew lonely, rotten stumps and broken withies.

The barge drifted nearer, her reflection playing idly before the bluff bows, and her dinghy following on the end of a heavy painter that drooped in the middle to the surface. As the stately old vessel glided past within a few yards of *Swan* the elderly skipper left the wheel and stood against the rail, hands in pockets, surveying the unfamiliar little barge yacht ... We exchanged greetings ... And when the barge had gone and only the masts and patched tanned sails appeared over the sedge grass of the unnamed islet, I stripped in the well ... and dived into the limpid depths of the creek. And everywhere silence reigned, the silence of big open spaces, of Nature at her best, of the – creeks ...

Reading those passages again, decades later, I reflected about the barge. Was she, I wondered, the same barge that lies rotting in the saltings at the head of Beaumont Creek, where only the skeleton of her hull now remains?

The Backwaters are a unique area of some 5,000 acres forming a huge bay of tidal creeks, islands and saltings tucked away from the sea, with one navigable channel at its entrance. Although much of the region is remote and accessible only by water, there are a number of public footpaths and sea-wall walks skirting the limits of waterway and marsh where the rambler can observe something of its character.

Remarkably, the natural features of the area have changed little, if at all, from Maurice Griffiths' early sailing days or from the picture Arthur Ransome drew in his *Secret Water*, which appeared in 1939 – except, of course, there are now many more boats and a huge marina just west of Walton town to serve them. But most of the yachts are in evidence only during the sailing season. In autumn, winter and spring, Hamford Water and the creeks, islands and saltings that run off it to the north and west belong almost exclusively to the wildlife and flora. These are the

Footpaths across the Saltings

seasons in which the Backwaters resume their remote and lonely character.

Like many other places of outstanding natural interest, the Backwaters and the country immediately surrounding them would not have retained their unique character if it were not for the conservation organizations that defend such areas from exploitation midst the rapid development of the south-east in recent years. It is not surprising that the Backwaters, together with the surrounding landscape, have for some time been a National Nature Reserve, recognized internationally for its exceptional observation qualities. The various national and local organizations concerned with their protection – the Essex Naturalists' Trust, Nature Conservancy Council, Tendring District Council, to name three – sponsor a warden service with the stated objective of promoting a better understanding of the area, enforcing local byelaws, reducing conflicts and safeguarding the environment.

Frank Bloom, a retired RNLI coxswain of the Walton lifeboat who, being a naturalist himself, has the aptitude for this interesting and demanding task, makes regular patrols, which also take in the shoreline, in his motor launch, and covers his routine observation of wildlife – recording arrivals and counts of visiting birds and geese as well as the welfare of the more permanent residents. Neither does the seasons' influence on the abundant plant life escape his attention, and when talking to him about his work I always get the impression that the Backwaters have become his second home.

'The saltmarsh to me is like a garden,' he says. 'It's always changing in colour; few realize the variety of flowers that grow there.'

He is a natural fund of local knowledge, and his friendly advice is always available to the visiting yachtsman or the naturalist or rambler who may chance to contact him.

Without the efforts of the counservationists, your views from the water and the sea walls would not be as unspoiled as they are today. The background of the country rising from sea-level as seen from a boat or a vantage-point on Horsey or Skippers Islands forms an escarpment for most of the way from the village of Little Oakley in the north on the Harwich–Thorpe road to the Naze cliffs at Walton in the east. From various vantage-points along these heights, the physical appearance of the whole area is seen as a huge, shallow basin of vegetation and water.

The countryside forming this gentle sweep down from the highways to the sea walls is farming land and in co-operation with landowners and other residents has been designated a Special

Landscape Area and thus will remain free from any development.

While your best observations of the reserve may be gained from a shallow-draft boat, the sea-wall walks provide an excellent platform for studying its topography and wildlife. Although on some sections of the wall there are no rights of way, there are a number of footpaths and other access points from the road which offer extensive walks round much of the area, albeit some of them are rough and overgrown in places. These access points are located at Little Oakley, Beaumont Quay, Landermere, Kirby-le-Soken and Walton.

One of the best vantage-points is, of course, the Naze or Ness, which means 'nose' in Old English, at the northern end of the town. Here, from the car-park in the shadow of the Naze Tower, between a small cluster of modern flats, there are glimpses westward over most of the Backwaters. The highest point of the Naze cliffs is some seventy-five feet above sea-level; they constitute the only true cliffs along the Essex coast, an appropriate place on which to locate a beacon to shipping – which Trinity House did in 1720, when the Naze Tower was built. The extensive views to the north from here take in the entrance to Harwich harbour and the ferries and container shipping serving Felixstowe port and Harwich.

The old lifeboat house at Walton-on-the-Naze

Walton and Frinton Yacht Club

From the cliffs down to the sea walls the walks are leisurely and easy on the feet; the grass is short and the ground comparatively even, for the area of greensward and the paths leading down from it are maintained by the district council in co-operation with the Essex Naturalists' Trust to form the Naze Nature Trail.

Here you can see the results of coastal erosion which has taken place along the south-east coast for many centuries, as well as the geology of the cliffs. You are warned to keep away from the cliff edge, but from below you can see the different rock structures: boulder clays and gravels above red crag and London clay which forms the base, the latter dating back some 50 million years. A variety of fossils has been found on the beach, washed out by the tide from the London clay – shells, shark's teeth, ancient bird bones and copperas, a fossilized wood of ferrous sulphate which was collected during the eighteenth century and processed into a liquid for making black ink and dye for leather and cloth. The commonest fossilized shell is the whelk, which is similar to the modern whelk except that the coil winds the opposite way – anti-clockwise.

Certainly the Ness ran much further seaward in ancient times; flint tools have been washed ashore dating from the neolithic period, some 4,000 years ago. Erosion all along the coast is a continual process – the sea-level is said to be rising at the rate of one foot every hundred years. A medieval church which stood on the Naze cliffs collapsed into the sea in 1798; evidence of this progress in more recent years is seen in the shape of the two concrete bunkers that were built well back from the cliff top during the last war and which are now breaking up on the beach and awash at high tide. Similar examples can be found in various places right round the East Anglian coast.

The nature trail is devised to cover a number of different localities, all with their own particular species of wildlife and flora, amongst vegetation of gorse, elder trees and hawthorn hedges. From the cliff slope, apart from the views of Hamford Water to the west and Harwich and Felixstowe to the north, the vista ahead encompasses the little creeks and acres of saltings which extend from the mainland to the shingle spit of Stone Point at the entrance to the Backwaters.

The slope levels out at the sea-wall and overlooks a sandy beach which is the haunt in winter of flocks of sanderlings. West along the wall and on the seaward side is a large, reedy pool, a good place to see dunlin, shelduck, redshank and swans. The grasses around the walls are ungrazed and develop a number of flowering

The mill which stood on the yacht club site
during the eighteenth and nineteenth centuries

A skein of brent-geese

plants which attract a variety of butterflies. From here the wall offers a comfortable walk westward to Walton Channel, which can be followed back to the edge of the town.

Quite apart from the naturalists' interest, the scenic qualities of the Naze would be the most attractive part of any seaside town. It provides a striking contrast to Walton itself, whose centre is comparatively small and congested and seems even more so in the summer, when it becomes a popular resort with day-trippers and holidaymakers. Apart from the modern amusements and ice-cream parlours, the town still has a Victorian air about it. Its development as a 'bathing place' began with the Portobello Hotel, built in 1829, and the Marine Hotel which followed it; but it was the completion of the railway from Colchester in 1867 and the construction of the pier two years later that opened it up as a seaside resort and a port of call for the coastal steam-packet.

Like the steam-packets, the old hotels have long since gone, but the long pier remains as a holiday attraction and also serves the lifeboat which is moored closeby. This floating RNLI station was set up in 1900, with the arrival of a new craft to replace the beach-launched boat housed at the end of East Terrace. The Victorian brick-and-tiled lifeboat house with its first-floor bay 'look-out' window was built in 1884 to take the first RNLI boat, which was bought with funds raised by the Honourable Artillery Company, encamped in the area at the time. Through the efforts of the Frinton and Walton Heritage Trust, the old building has now been given a new lease of life as a maritime museum. As an ex-coxswain, Frank Bloom has played a leading role in converting the interior and organizing many of the exhibits, which include an old lobster beach-boat complete with lugsail and the renovation of the original RNLI boarding-boat which conveyed the crew from the pier to the lifeboat mooring. The museum, opened in the summer of 1989, provides an interesting contrast with the modern coastguard station next door.

The impression of Walton as a seaside resort remains very much as it was in pre-war days, although now the summer visitors tend to stay in caravans rather than hotels and boarding-houses.

I seldom go there without looking down Mill Lane, just off the High Street. It is the nearest point to the Backwaters from the town. Here the tidal creeks from Walton Channel and Foundry Reach fizzle out at the Town Hard. As its name implies, the lane ran to the mills that signify the other industries of Walton in the eighteenth and nineteenth centuries – milling and brewing. In those days the windmill and tidemill worked almost within a stone's throw of each other, an unusual combination that must have created keen competition.

Park the car alongside the embankment that overlooks the old

Skippers Island

mill pool and from the top you can see where the tidemill stood. A later building occupies the site now, and the old quay which served the sailing-barges has been replaced by a modern one, the present-day industry catering for the pleasure sailor and the fisherman. The area is occupied by boatyards, repair sheds, chandlers and boat-parks. The roadway continues through this complex to the head of the main channel, which divides into two creeks either side of it, where stands the Walton and Frinton Yacht Club, built in the early twenties on the site of the old postmill.

Mill Lane provides a glimpse of the delightful area from the town, but for the sea wall walks and the old barge quays near the tidal limits you need to go west, along the Walton Road to Kirby-le-Soken and beyond. This village, like Thorpe-le-Soken and ancient Walton, was granted the 'soke' or 'liberty' in feudal times which entitled it to run its own affairs, with private laws and other privileges.

The creeks penetrate here to the edge of the village, and a short walk down Quay Lane brings you to Kirby Quay and, just across the dike, the tarred, weatherboarded pilot's cottage with its red-brick chimney and thatched roof, a reminder of the trading days when the quay was busy with barge traffic. Across the dike, in the

A sluice on Skippers Island

Landermere

direction of Walton, the sea-wall will take you round to Island Lane and the gravel causeway which at low tide is the vehicle land-link with Horsey Island. This is a popular habitat for wildfowl and was one of the locations for the filming of Paul Gallico's *The Snow Goose*. The view across the Wade takes in the southern shoreline of the island with Kirby Creek to the north-west, and north-east across Twizzle Creek to Hedge End Island and the yacht masts of Titchmarsh marina.

Horsey Island is privately owned and covers about 500 acres, including the saltings; it is the largest of the archipelago. The land is farmed organically by the owners, Mrs Backhouse and her son, who are keen conservationists. It is mainly pasture, with hedge-lined grazing fields and sheltered pools for wildfowl. The owners are well known for their Arab horses, which are bred on the island and which, with flocks of sheep, keep the grasses close-cropped for the benefit of the brent-geese. When I was there in early February, the fields were alive with flapping wings and the honking calls of a large proportion of the 3,000 brent that migrate to the Backwaters each year. Amongst other species I saw were greylag and Canada geese, black-headed gulls, avocets and snipe.

From the north shore of Horsey, across Hamford Water, is Oakley Creek. From the broad entrance the creek winds up

A 'stackie'

between Bramble and Peewit islands, and although the channel narrows between saltings and mudflats in the higher reaches, small coasters use the wharf on Bramble Island, which serves the explosives factory located there. There is ample water within the entrance of the creek, but anchoring is not recommended, as these coasters move in and out at any time of the day or night. Landing on Bramble Island is strictly prohibited.

Horsey Island is certainly a splendid observatory for the naturalist, but no landing should be made without prior permission of the owners. This also applies to Skippers Island, just across Kirby Creek, a reserve of over 200 acres owned by the Essex Naturalists' Trust, whose headquarters are based at the Fingringhoe Wick Nature Reserve, overlooking the River Colne a few miles from Colchester. Access to Skippers Island obviously has to be arranged well in advance: apart from the fact that the creek system can be crossed on foot only at low water, or by boat at other states of the tide, the route from the road is privately owned.

I found the layout of Skippers Island very different from Horsey – apart from its being less than half the size – in that it is really a complex of three islands, connected by sea walls with numerous creeks and large areas of mudflats and saltmarsh. You can see something of its contours from the observation tower which overlooks the principal land habitats of scrub and coastal grasslands. To the west of the landing-area is the heronry, with old elms, elder and some silver birch, and a nearby fresh-water pool and salt-water lagoon whose level is controlled by a sluice to suit different bird species at different times of the year. Both the resident and migrating bird populations are supported by the mudflats and saltmarsh, and in the main island thickets there are several species of warbler, a recent colonist being the nightingale.

Lieutenant-Colonel Hawkes, the resident warden, is another naturalist whose enthusiasm ensures the smooth running of the reserve. I thought a continuous problem must be the maintenance of the sea walls, particularly during winter, with tidal surges and gale-force winds liable to cause a breech; but I had the feeling that, if there *was* a problem, it sat lightly enough on his shoulders. I wondered, too, if he ever felt cut off, isolated, but after hours ranging the reserve in his company and learning something of his daily routines, I realized he would not have time to feel lonely.

West from here, along Walton Road, a lane leads down to Landermere Quay. The land, foreshore, wharf and saltings are privately owned but there is footpath access along the lane and from the sea walls. Landermere is a pretty little haven with one or two houses tucked away behind the trees, a small beach and the

Rose, *a derelict barge at Beaumont Quay*

An old warehouse at Beaumont Quay

remains of the old barge wharf which overlooks Landermere creek and the entrance to Beaumont Cut. This narrow waterway penetrates to Beaumont Quay, which is an easy sea-wall walk of less than a mile from Landermere.

All these old quays near the tidal limits adjoined farming land, for the cargoes here were related mainly to agriculture, and some of the sailing-barges were owned by farmers or agents in the trade. Their main cargoes were hay and straw for the London horses, their return load manure or 'muck', which was the usual term for fertilizer from London stables. The 'stackies', as these craft were called, designed to carry such huge loads, were often smaller than the general traders, since they had to worm their way up the narrowest creeks and gutways to load and unload at the fieldside quays. Navigating these craft (sixty feet or more in length) under sail in such confined waters with a stack on deck a quarter the height of the mast required remarkable skill, even with the mate atop the stack directing his skipper. These barges also carried other cargoes – grain, timber, bricks – most of the requirements of the farming community. And they were still trading under sail in this fashion until the last war.

The remains of one stackie you can see for yourself at Beaumont

Quay. Her skeleton lies rotting in the saltings at the head of the creek. She was the *Rose*, Maldon-based, and her most recent history suggests she was sold there in 1961/2 and brought round to Beaumont at that time; but I could not discover how she came to be abandoned.

Another remnant of the period is the old warehouse still standing close to the quay which has an inscribed tablet let into the wall which informs you that stone used in the building of the quay in 1832 came from the old London Bridge built around 1176.

This BUILDING and QUAY
was Erected by the
VERNORS of GUYS HOSPITA
1832
HARRISON Esq. Treasurer
The Stone used in the Quay formed part
of LONDON BRIDGE built about
1176

Beaumont Quay has close access to the Harwich–Thorpe road. A short lane takes you down to the farm, where a footpath leads onto the sea-wall and back to Landermere.

Each quay has its own fascination, but an interesting historical feature at Landermere is the terrace of cottages a few yards along the lane from the wharf. Gull Cottages are said to take their name from an early occupant, Sir William Withey Gull, who became an eminent physician late in the last century, attending the Court of Queen Victoria at the time of the 'Jack the Ripper' murders. Some records of the time seem to link Gull's name with these crimes, and in recent years books on the subject and a television dramatization of the Whitechapel murders have suggested Gull as being a leading suspect; it is a fascinating historical case for the criminologist, but there appears to be no hard evidence to support the theory. We do know, however, that Gull was a great benefactor in the local parish, supporting charitable trusts and the church of St Michael's in Thorpe-le-Soken, the village in which he spent much of his childhood. He died in 1890 and was buried, at his own wish, in the village churchyard.

More than a century earlier the village and church were the setting for the climax of a more romantic story, which appears in the records as the strange but true tale of Kitty Canham. Most

Gull Cottages, Landermere

books on Essex refer to this pretty, vivacious character who helped her mother run the grocery store, and who became the wife of the Revd Henry Gough, newly appointed incumbent, a man many years her senior.

After three years of marriage Kitty, unable to accept the quiet, unexciting life of the vicarage, ran away to London. Four years later, in 1752, a small ship from the Continent bound for Harwich was driven off course in a storm and put into the Colne. The preventive officers, always alert for smugglers, boarded the vessel and immediately took an interest in a large crate belonging to the only passenger, listed as a Mr Williams, merchant of Hamburg. Other items – female accessories and jewellery – were found in Williams' luggage, and the officers ordered him to open the crate. After much protesting, the agitated man did so, to reveal a silver-embellished coffin and, inside, the embalmed body of a beautiful woman.

The officers, suspecting murder, took the vessel to Hythe Quay

and left the situation in the hands of the nonplussed Colchester
authorities. They locked up the coffin and Williams in the vestry
of the parish church. Amongst the sightseers who came to witness
this scene was a man who recognized Kitty, and he hurried to
Thorpe to inform Gough of his wife's mysterious return. Gough,
complete with sword, rode to Colchester and confronted
Williams, who confessed his true identity and related the series of
events that had brought him and the body of Kitty to Britain.

He was Lord Dalmeny, and he had met the beautiful girl in
London four years before, fallen in love with her and, assuming
she was free to marry, gone through the ceremony, then taken her
to the Continent, where he had spent most of his time. But his
social life there did not suit her health, and she fell ill and died in
Verona. Before she died, Kitty confessed her bigamy and implored
Dalmeny to take her body back to Thorpe to be buried in the
churchyard of her home village.

Dalmeny's confession dispelled Gough's bewilderment and
anger, and he accepted the explanation. The two men became

St Mary's, Thorpe-le-Soken

reconciled and walked together at the funeral. Dalmeny never married and died three years later, at the age of thirty-one. Henry Gough resumed his quiet life in the village and lived another twenty years.

A highly romantic story and one that should interest the historical novelist – if it has not already done so.

The past is patterned with tales of romance, smuggling, torture and murder and, like other parts of the country, East Anglia has its share of stories, myths and legends. One of the more gruesome events, which occurred over a hundred years before Kitty Canham's romantic adventure, took place a few miles from Thorpe, on the Essex–Suffolk border at the head of the Stour estuary. On the edge of Constable Country ... But more of this later.

2

Constable's River

The broad sweep of the Stour estuary narrows to a placid, reed-fringed river above Manningtree and the Cattawade barrage ten miles up from Harwich, winding its way through the valley to the old lock at Flatford Mill into the heart of Constable Country. 'I associate my careless boyhood to all that lies on the banks of the Stour,' Constable wrote. 'They made me a painter.'

The banks of the Stour and the surrounding countryside from Flatford to Stoke-by-Nayland and beyond will always be synonymous with the artist's name, but the Stour estuary and Harwich at its mouth were also the setting for a number of his marine studies, although Harwich itself is perhaps better known for other famous characters from the past – Samuel Pepys, Captain Christopher Jones of the *Mayflower* and, of course, Nelson.

One glimpse of the old streets of Harwich and you will be back in the past. Your surroundings cannot fail to evoke the atmosphere of a medieval trading-port which became a major centre for shipbuilding as well as an early naval base. One glance at its position on the map and you can see why it has always featured as a bastion of the country's front-line defences in times of war.

Harwich stands on a small peninsula pushing out into the confluent estuaries of the Stour and Orwell. It looks east across the harbour to the container port of Felixstowe, north into the mouth of the Orwell and west up the Stour. As any visitor will rapidly appreciate, Harwich is almost surrounded by water!

The Harwich Skyline

Parkeston Quay, the well-known passenger terminal for the Continent, is about a mile up the Stour from Harwich, with direct access to the quayside by rail and road, so that passengers miss the opportunity of passing through Harwich town. Whenever I have taken the North Sea ferry and we have slipped past Harwich quay, I have often wondered if any of my deck companions have any idea of the port's distinguished history and the fascination of its streets and buildings. Could any visualize, for instance, as we ploughed slowly out of the bustling harbour, that in 1588 the English fleet had sailed in after the defeat of the Armada or that the *Mayflower* which took the Pilgrim Fathers to America in 1602 was a Harwich vessel whose captain lived a few yards from the quay. You can see reminders of these and other past events all over Harwich, and a good place to start is the quay, where there are a couple of dozen parking-slots and views across the river to Shotley on the Suffolk side.

The quay, which is at the end of the main thoroughfare, West Street, runs between Trinity Pier to your left and Navyard Wharf to the right. In between is Ha'penny Pier (so called because of the halfpenny toll), which was a busy calling-point for paddle-steamers until after the First World War. Nowadays the small ferries to Felixstowe and Shotley operate from here, the latter service recently starting again after a lapse of thirty years, with the opening of the Shotley Point marina, where passengers board and disembark. Incidentally, a notable feature at the pier is the ticket

office. The small circular building with its bell-shaped roof complete with bell cage was the first Continental booking-office and is a good example of late nineteenth-century architecture.

Between the pier and Navyard Wharf is the Pound where the pilot boats and the lifeboat were moored. These craft now operate from the pier of the Harwich Haven Authority at Navigation House, facing the quays of Felixstowe port across the harbour. The Pound is now practically deserted but for one or two small craft and a few fishing-boats that can usually be found alongside the quay.

The latest development at the eastern end of the quay is the roll-on/roll-off terminal at Navyard Wharf established by the Harwich Dock Company in 1962 on what was originally a naval shipyard where many fine men-of-war were built during the seventeenth, eighteenth and nineteenth centuries. In the early days the diarist Samuel Pepys was a familiar figure there; he was secretary of the Admiralty as well as being MP for Harwich and was a friend of fellow-MP Anthony Deane, who designed many of the vessels that were built there. A complete list of the ships is displayed at the dock gates and makes impressive reading. The yard was run by a number of different owners in later years. Before the last war it was busy with ship-repair work and maintenance, and I remember seeing sailing-barges and other vessels on the slips in the 1930s. During the war it no doubt served the Admiralty again, for during that time Harwich harbour was once more a naval base.

Harwich ferry ticket-office

Harwich has also been a base for Trinity House since 1912 and is now the main depot in England, supervising operations all round the country from its control headquarters on the quay and servicing the lighthouses, light vessels and buoys along the east coast.

The Trinity House Lighthouse Service goes back to 1514, and about a hundred years later the pilotage of shipping, beginning with the Thames, came under its control. The expansion of the pilotage districts followed, and for some 400 years the corporation was responsible for the pilotage service, but control has now been transferred to the harbour boards and authorities in the various areas.

In 1988 the Harwich Haven Authority took on pilotage responsibilities for the Haven Ports of Felixstowe, Harwich, Ipswich and Mistley, and the pilot boats operate from the authority's pier on the east side of the town. With some 24,000 shipping movements in the harbour approaches annually, these small, distinguished craft with their black hulls and orange-coloured superstructures can be seen speeding in and out of the harbour at all times of the day.

Apart from the transfer of pilotage, Trinity House has also been changing its operating methods – including the use of helicopters, taking advantage of the developing automation of the technological age. The manned light vessel, employing a crew of five, has become obsolete. Most of these are now monitored and controlled from headquarters, and two of them are off Harwich on the *Sunk* and *Shipwash* stations. Others can be seen in the harbour awaiting or undergoing conversion. Some lightships have been sold – they can be turned into spacious clubhouses – the one at the Suffolk Yacht Harbour on the Orwell housing the Haven Ports Yacht Club is a particularly good example. Others have been replaced by the LANBY (Large Automatic Navigation Buoy) which is in fact a circular platform with a short mast topped by an automatically operated light. One or more of these buoys, weighing ninety-five tons when fully laden with water ballast and fuel, can usually be found moored in the harbour during their service intervals.

There is always a huddle of buoys peeping over the walls of the maintenance yard and some on Trinity Pier, and with their varied shapes, sizes and colours they will be the first objects to draw your attention when you turn out of West Street onto the quay. I have never failed to find something of interest going on here: small boats, fishing-boats, coming and going, a tug thrusting her way up river, the harbour ferry leaving Ha'penny Pier, a lighthouse tender alongside Trinity Pier, a North Sea ferry outward bound or one heading slowly up the Stour to Parkeston Quay and, on occasion, the arrival of the 2,500-ton *Patricia*, the impressive flagship of Trinity House.

Obsolete light vessel off Parkston Quay

The most imposing building on the quay is the nineteenth-century Great Eastern Hotel, its flamboyant design typical of the grandiose style that can be found in many such buildings of the period. In face of the limited berthing facilities at Harwich, it was too ambitious a project to be viable for long, and it turned out to be a white elephant so far as the Great Eastern Railway Company was concerned.

The railway arrived in Harwich before the hotel was built, with a line along the quay and another running on to the Railway Pier (now Trinity Pier), where the Continental packets berthed, so the hotel served its purpose until the passenger traffic increased and the ships became larger and the port facilities could no longer cope. Moreover, there was a sad lack of harmony between the Harwich authorities and the railway company over the use of the limited water and quay space; in any event, with no way of expanding the facilities to accommodate the new ships, the GER was forced to look elsewhere.

The building of Parkeston Quay (named after Charles Parkes, the then chairman of the GER), together with its hotel and housing development for the railway workers, is fully documented elsewhere; suffice to say that this successful venture eliminated all viability of the grand hotel on Harwich Quay, and its ownership passed to the borough council. Since then it has served many uses: the Admiralty took it over during the two world wars, and after the second it became the town hall, was used as council offices and is now an apartment block.

Although Harwich declined through the loss of its Continental traffic, it resumed its association with the railway in 1924, when the LNER opened its daily train ferry services to Zeebrugge from a new terminal next to Trinity Pier, and this operated until 1987, when it was transferred to Dover. The lines still run to the terminal but the only immediate reminder of the ferry is the tall metal structure of the lifting-gantry.

The tidal inlet just beyond the terminal is Gas House Creek, where a few fishing-boats lie and where the Harwich and Dovercourt Sailing Club is located. Looking at the creek now, it is not difficult to imagine how it appeared around the turn of the century, when it was the site of J. and H. Cann's yard, a family firm who built some of the finest Thames sailing-barges between 1880 and 1914.

Although sadly there is little to show here that recalls the heyday of the sailorman, on a walk through the town along the narrow streets from the quay you will find reminders of the old port with almost every step.

For too long Harwich appeared to be a neglected, unattractive place with apparently little effort and initiative by those in authority to take advantage of its potential as a tourist attraction as well as restoring its appearance for the benefit of its residents; but in recent years this attitude has changed, and now its cobbled streets are tidier, old buildings have been – and continue to be – meticulously restored and there is an air about it all that suggests that the town is worth showing to the visitor. And so it is.

Most of this is due to the work and enthusiasm of the Harwich Society, many members of which, living in the town, have restored their own properties. The society set out to enhance the town's image and promote its historical links with the sea, and this they continue to do successfully. Apart from restoration, other aspects of their activities can be seen in the informative plaques erected on significant buildings, the planting of trees, the creation of a maritime museum and the issue of a number of illustrated publications to steer the visitor around.

Winifred Cooper, a founder member and present chairman of the society, who lives in Church Street in what is thought to be the oldest house in the town, tells me that from the early days of the society's formation in 1969 they had no co-operation from the authorities or other bodies, and it was left to the few enthusiastic members with little finance actively to promote their objectives in making the Harwich area (including the adjoining resort of Dovercourt) a better place to live in.

Although it was a lone struggle at the beginning, in the last few years the national emphasis on conservation has brought in new members and has resulted in the growing support, both moral and financial, of the relevant councils and other organizations – although, like similar voluntary bodies, the society is always in need of funds.

'Maybe,' Winifred Cooper says, 'at a future date it will be said, as did Elizabeth I, that Harwich is "a pretty town and wants nothing".'

The Low Lighthouse, at the edge of the green overlooking the east beach, was opened as a maritime museum in 1980; but the society's most ambitious project is the restoration of the Redoubt, the huge Napoleonic fort on Tower Hill between the Dovercourt road and Harbour Crescent. The Redoubt formed part of the Martello chain of defences which extend from Aldeburgh to Seaford. It is an impressive fortification, 200 feet in diameter, with a central parade eighty-five feet across and walls three feet thick, and was armed with ten 24-pounder cannon. It had its own water supply from a well in the centre of the parade, and up to 300 men

The Low Lighthouse, Harwich

could be sustained in siege conditions. Members began restoration soon after the society was formed; work is still under way, and it is now the largest ancient monument in the country being restored by a voluntary group.

If the Redoubt is the prize feature of the society's work, evidence of their increasing influence is apparent in the town, particularly in the number of houses that have been restored. Winifred Cooper's house is a fine example which she and her late husband restored as early as 1953. Of timber frame and plaster construction, it was built in 1450, later served as an ale-house and from 1800 to 1940 traded as the Foresters Arms. It is now a very comfortable private home with many of its original interior features revealed and enhanced, sensitively evoking the atmosphere of the period.

Harwich has many old inns, some with early associations of smuggling, not an unusual feature of any ancient seafaring town. Just along the street, in the shadow of St Nicholas' Church, whose tall spire dominates the town and is a landmark from the harbour approaches, is the Three Cups, a sixteenth-century hostelry in which many famous names were entertained in the past. In 1753 sea-water baths were introduced, an innovation typical of a number of seaside resorts from the early days to the Victorian era, and the yard of the Three Cups, now an open car-park, rattled to the sound of horses' hoofs and coaches depositing visitors to take the cure. Its records recall that Nelson stayed there in 1801, and legend has it that Lady Hamilton accompanied him.

Another notable event which took place there was the foundation of the Royal Harwich Yacht Club in September 1843, during the Harwich Regatta Dinner. The club remained in the town until 1946, when it moved to a more spacious site at Cat House Hard, Woolverstone, some eight miles up the Orwell estuary from Harwich.

Some of the more elegant houses in the town were owned by the richest people – the ships' captains. Harwich has been the home of many master mariners through the centuries, but the most famous of them was Captain Christopher Jones, master of the *Mayflower*, whose finely restored house is just off the quay in Kings Head Street.

It may come as a surprise to find that an old seafaring town like Harwich should have the earliest of associations with the cinema, but Friese Green, the inventor of cinematography, lived there at one time, and in Kings Quay Street is the oldest unchanged purpose-built cinema in Britain. Dating from 1911, the Electric

Foresters, said to be the oldest house in Harwich (c. 1450)

A glimpse of old Harwich

Palace (restored to its former glory by the Harwich Electric Palace Trust, a sister organization of the Harwich Society and reopened in 1981), was built for an East Anglian showman, and this is evident in its ornate front, which displays all the influence of the showground.

Just east of the cinema, adjoining the green, are the dinghy park and clubhouse of the Harwich Town Sailing Club, and on the green itself a quaint relic from the naval shipyard, the Treadwheel Crane, built in 1667, which was operated by men walking in the interior of the two wheels. With the crude form of braking available at the time (a spar levered against the outer edge of the wheel), it must have been a hair-raising occupation. The crane is believed to be the only example of its kind in Britain.

Two features that will attract your attention either end of the green are the High and Low Lighthouses. These two monuments with their canopied tops were the leading lights to guide shipping in through the harbour channel, but within a few years the direction of the channel was affected by shifting shoals, and the lights eventually became known as 'misleading lights'. To replace them, two iron lighthouses were erected on Dovercourt sea-front, but these were discontinued for the same reason in 1917 and the channel was then marked by lighted buoys. The two light towers on iron legs are listed buildings and have now been preserved and form part of the maritime heritage of the two towns.

From Dovercourt's Marine Parade, with its statue of Queen Victoria to greet you as you come up the main thoroughfare from the town centre, you have uninterrupted views of the harbour approaches and the long arm of the stone breakwater below Beacon Cliff which overlooks the harbour entrance. This is the location for a proposed marina, most of it to be built on reclaimed land on the foreshore on the Harwich side of the breakwater. 'Sportport' is a £50 million project whose plans include a thousand-berth yacht harbour with workshops, over 300 homes, a hotel and a supermarket. While the new marina would give easy access to coastwise sailors, as its position would be well away from the shipping channel in the harbour, the approach by road through the confined town centre of Dovercourt would cause immense congestion problems. However, plans are afoot to bypass the town centre by extending the Colchester road from the Parkeston roundabout to Harwich Quay. Certainly some improvement in the road network needs to be done before the completion of the marina complex – whenever that is likely to be.

The Treadwheel Crane, Harwich

But once through Upper Dovercourt and heading west for the village of Ramsey you soon lose any feeling of congestion. Cross the Colchester highway and through the village, overlooked by a restored post-windmill, and you are on a country road (B1352) which runs parallel with the Stour estuary from Ramsey to Manningtree; tortuous and in places presenting a switchback impression, it offers wide and intermittent views of the river, with the waterside villages of Wrabness and Bradfield *en route*.

The High Lighthouse, Harwich

My first stop on this road would be Stour Wood, a mile or so from Ramsey and less than that from Wrabness. It is mainly of oak and sweet chestnut, and I remember in my early days the extensive chestnut coppice being worked, the trade continuing until the mid 1970s. The wood is now an RSPB reserve, with a convenient car-park just off the road, and two waymarked paths down to a hide on the edge of the estuary providing views of Copperas Bay. The woodland is a habitat for a variety of bird-life, including the nightingale, and in autumn, winter and spring the mudflats, saltmarsh and reedbeds are the feeding-grounds for the usual flocks of wildfowl and waders that are among the great attractions of the East Anglian estuaries.

But the best view of Copperas Bay is from the high ground on the north side of Wrabness village. From the pub opposite the station approach, the lane over the railway bridge ends in two footpaths: the nearer one, following the railway cutting and skirting the wood, reaches the shore beside an isolated cottage; the other goes direct across farming land to the river bank. From their highest points the wide view down river to Parkeston Quay covers most of the bay, and at low tide the enormous extent of the mudflats can be appreciated. Above Parkeston the channel hugs the Suffolk shore before turning back to the Essex side, providing deep-water moorings for boats close to Wrabness beach.

You can reach the east end of the beach via the path from the village which follows the bank up river, moves onto the sea-wall past Shore Farm and brings you out at the end of a private lane. This used to be the access for Shore Farm, for moving implements and cattle; it has for many years been the access to the chalets which line the beach and most of Wrabness cliff. The meadow, too, adjoining the lane, where as a boy I was forced up a tree to avoid the bull, has a fringe of holiday caravans within its boundary hedge.

In my earliest days when I first spent time there, the beach was as deserted as the proverbial desert isle, and apart from a couple of small chalets at the extreme western end and on occasion a visiting yacht or two anchored just off the cliff, nothing changed

Old iron lighthouses, Dovercourt

the atmosphere of the natural environment. Hall Farm, topping the rising ground and fronting the village road, was a source of milk and eggs for campers near the shore, who just helped themselves to water from the pump in the yard.

The sandy beach was a remote playground that gently shelved into a muddy hard and at low tide shelved again towards the channel where the soft mud sucked around the feet and one often sank in to one's knees. It was a good place to learn to handle a small boat; a good place to learn to swim. The water was clean and, on a calm day, clear. Under the sun the hot mud lifted the temperature of the incoming tide, and swimming in the shallows was like taking a warm bath. No one associated pollution with salt water when I first unintentionally took a mouthful. And when the tide was at its lowest, there was always the mud. All East Anglian estuaries wallow in it. Estuarine mud; a cold, brown mass under a grey sky, a glistening surface of pewter throwing back the light of the sun with here and there a mirror-streak of water trapped in its folds, dazzling the eye. Mud, often as warm and as gooey to the touch as buttered toast, was, it used to be said, very beneficial to aching feet. Mine were, of course, too young to ache in those days.

The scene is different now. The Hall is a non-farming residence and, with its timbered barn and other buildings which distance the house from the church, may, I am told, become a health farm. Most of the land has been sold off in lots, which I hope will not result in some future developments that further change the shape of this pretty slice of undulating countryside.

The estuary here is over a mile wide (for most of its length the shores are around this distance apart), with the mudflats running out from Holbrook Creek. Crowning the rising ground above the creek are the long, low buildings and spire of the Royal Hospital School, the first object to attract the eye since it appears an unusual intrusion amongst the villages, halls, farmlands and wooded country on the Suffolk side.

The channel swings away again at the western end of Wrabness beach towards the northern shore, leaving at low tide another vast expanse of mudflats that fill Jaques Bay. At the beach end is a lane that gives the only public car access to Wrabness shore, and here the sea wall resumes again and offers a walk of a mile or so to Bradfield beach. Here there is another public access which will take you into Bradfield village.

Bradfield is an old agricultural village with some residential expansion and was the home of Sir Harbottle Grimston, who became the local MP and played a leading role in Parliament in the mid seventeenth century.

Another mile west and you are in Mistley, with its tree-shaded riverside Strand linking it to Manningtree. The channel curves in again alongside Mistley Quay, then out again and round to the old timber wharf at Manningtree, which dries out at low water.

The two ports were significant maritime trading-stations in past centuries, and although Manningtree's trade declined, Mistley has always retained its importance in the coasting trade. The yard at the eastern end of the quays was once associated with the name of Horlock, the family who maintained and sailed a working fleet of well-known sailing-barges over many years; it is now a small shipbreaker's yard. Mistley port has expanded in recent times and has become one of the best equipped of the small east-coast ports, a development no doubt due in the main to Britain's entry into the European Community. Many small freighters now use the quays, and with the further dredging of the channel it will eventually be possible to accommodate ships of 5,000 tons. The port handles grain, timber and stone, and gravel which is dredged from the channel; but the principal industry there is – as it has been since the eighteenth century – malting. The tall buildings with their ventilated tops are the first to catch the eye whether one approaches from the river or by road downhill to the square.

The farmlands of East Anglia have always produced the finest malting barley, and still do, although now it is moved by mechanical power whereas in the past it arrived at the quayside granaries by barge or horse-drawn wagon, and the malt conveyed in sailing-barges to the London breweries.

Mistley Quay

Much of Mistley still displays the influence of the Rigbys, a wealthy eighteenth-century family who built much of the town and the waterfront. When Richard Rigby inherited his father's estates and came to live at Mistley, he built himself Mistley Hall, a sumptuous place in keeping with his pompous and flamboyant character. The grounds of the Hall, which border the Strand opposite the river, were landscaped in an elaborate style; the only reminder now of past grandeur is an ornamental lake which can be seen from the road.

Rigby was a great socializer, and amongst his friends was Robert Adam, whom he called in to design a salt-water bath-house close to the river, his intention being to promote Mistley as a spa. A start was made but the ambition was never realized, and all that remain of this enterprise are the swan fountain and pavilion in the square. More prominent monuments to Adam's design can be seen in the two Mistley Towers at the entry to the Strand, sole remnants of the old Mistley Thorn church. Rigby's plan was to enhance the red-brick church so that its appearance was more in keeping with the ornate trimmings of his estate. The results of Adam's work were two square towers at each end of the church, embellished by porticoes with Tuscan columns. When dry rot caused the church to be demolished in 1870 and replaced with the Victorian church along the road, the towers were left as 'mausoleums', although they were never used for this purpose. They stand now as empty curios, in contrast to

Mistley Towers

the modern quayside warehouses nearby. The Rigby estates were sold up in 1844, and a year later Mistley Hall was demolished, although one of the two lodges Adam built in 1782 still survives at the junction of the Clacton–Mistley–Colchester roads.

Further attractive features of the Strand and Mistley quays are the swans. For many years there has been a large population here, attracted by the grain cargoes and the maltings. They congregate in the channel below the wharves and along the riverbank, where the green sward of the Strand is popular with visitors, who can often be seen feeding the swans.

Manningtree, until the boundary changes, was the smallest town in England. The narrow streets are shadowed by many Georgian façades that conceal early Tudor or Elizabethan houses. Much of the town's wealth in those days was derived from the cloth industry, and there are some fine examples of weavers' cottages in the streets running off the town centre.

Two old coaching inns with arched entrances to their stable yards, the White Hart and the Crown, are in the High Street. The yard of the Crown exits onto the short waterfront, and next to it the Stour Sailing Club is a hive of activity during the sailing season when the tide creeps in over the mudflats. Off the beach a variable fleet of small craft – yachts, fishing-boats, dinghies and two or three wildfowling gun punts – now takes the place of the commercial shipping of previous centuries when Manningtree was a thriving port. Upstream from the timber wharf one of the old maltings has been given a new lease of life in the shape of residential apartments, and new 'retirement' flats near the waterfront have been designed to harmonize with the period architecture.

The town has become a busy commercial centre again, with an industrial estate at its western fringe that has been developed in recent years. It seems difficult to associate it now with one of the most gruesome of medieval activities – witch-hunting, but in the seventeenth century, during the English Civil War, it became synonymous with the name of Matthew Hopkins, the Witchfinder General.

Hopkins was paid 20 shillings for each witch he successfully prosecuted, and his methods gave no chance to any suspect who fell victim to his accusations. Any woman he suspected of trading with the devil was tried by 'swimming'. Her hands and feet were tied, and she was lowered into a pool of water. If she drowned, she was not guilty; if she survived, she was convicted and hanged, so the unfortunate victim lost out either way. It is not known how many women he put to death, but it is reckoned to have been some hundreds, for he later operated in other towns in East Anglia. Hopkins was said to be a lawyer who lived in Manningtree and began his notorious work there. Some suggest that his headquarters was in the White Hart, but Russell Edwards, in his comprehensive book *The River Stour*, records that Hopkins 'held court' in Mistley at the Thorn Inn overlooking the square. He goes on to say that Hopkins' ghost is reputed to haunt the inn and, in fact, in his book he reproduces a photograph he took late one winter's afternoon in the courtyard in which can be seen a shadowy figure under the archway; but whether this is an apparition or a lighting fluke remains undecided. 'I think myself,' Russell Edwards concludes, 'that some trick of the light and a series of coincidences had been responsible for the uncanny image.'

The belief in witches and other evil influences was widely prevalent in medieval times, and the evidence of various practices to protect homes from these unnatural intrusions have been found during the restoration of old houses. Witch bottles, mummified cats and even horse skulls are some examples discovered that were sealed in the building near a chimney or under the floor during its construction to deter witches and evil spirits. I know of one seventeenth-century house in Suffolk where during restoration a mummified cat was discovered in the timber-framed part of the building. It was respectfully reinterred elsewhere.

Cattawade Barrage

Just above Manningtree the railway and road bridges cross the Stour at Cattawade, and the Stour valley opens up. The old red-brick arched road bridge has been replaced by a single span, and adjoining it downstream is the Cattawade Barrage, where large sluice gates regulate the outflow of the river into the tidal reaches and exclude sea water from penetrating further inland. On the Suffolk side, close to the old road bridge at Brantham, ramps and rollers have been installed giving access at high water to the river from the tidal estuary (and vice versa) for light craft.

The plastics factory at Brantham on the Suffolk bank of the estuary regrettably interrupts the views down river; but there has been an industrial plant here since before the turn of the century. Referred to locally as 'the Xylonite factory' or 'BX', it is now owned by ICI. I have always felt the sprawling complex an unfortunate intrusion just where the beautiful Stour valley merges with the estuary; but you may just as well regret the passing of the old bridge or Brantham Mill. Progress sweeps on, with the intention of economically benefiting the areas concerned; the consolation here is that the valley upstream remains very much as it has always been.

This is footpath country. From Cattawade to Flatford you have a choice of following the river up the valley on the Essex side or taking the path a short distance along the East Bergholt road on the Brantham side of the bridge. Here you pass the site of the old mill, with the lock just upstream. This was the limit of the Stour navigation from Sudbury when a variety of cargoes was moved up and down river in horse-drawn barges. At Brantham the horses were unharnessed and the barges floated on the tide down the estuary to Mistley Quay, no mean task in unsettled weather conditions.

The commercial navigation of the Stour came into operation early in the eighteenth century, when thirteen locks were constructed between Sudbury and Brantham, a distance of some twenty-four miles. At the head of navigation at Sudbury (where Gainsborough was born), a basin was built with quays and warehouses, and each mill on the river had its own wharf to accommodate the barges, which were over forty-five feet long and carried some thirteen tons of freight. The river traffic declined with the arrival of the railway (and, later, road transport), and the small riverside family mills were superseded by the milling companies. Commercial traffic ceased soon after the First World War, although the last barge was working to Dedham until 1928. The river, particularly the upper reaches, fell into decay. Various river boards and water authorities have been responsible for the

Brantham Lock (obsolete)

river over a number of years but their concerns were mainly its use in connection with water supplies. Weirs and sluices replaced many of the old locks, and few stretches remained navigable.

However, despite all the changes that have taken place since the river was made navigable by an Act of Parliament in 1705 (one of the country's earliest river navigations and presumably carrying traffic before that), it is still a statutory navigation. Even so, attempts were made to set aside the public right to navigate the river from Sudbury to the estuary, and to oppose these the River Stour Trust was set up in 1968. A registered charity allied to the Inland Waterways Association, the trust now has a strong supporting membership over a wide area, as well as within the Stour Valley, its policy being to protect and enhance the public right as well as the conservation of amenities and wildlife. Its interest in maintaining the navigation has allowed the use of the river by canoes and other small manually propelled craft, although these should be light enough for portage around weirs and other structures. Its objectives also include the removal of existing obstructions and the repair and restoration of the locks. Since its inception, the trust has made remarkable progress in this direction, and some of its work can be seen in the restoration of the lock and dry dock at Flatford, undertaken in collaboration with the National Trust.

Flatford Mill, owned by Golding Constable, the artist's father, together with Willy Lott's Cottage and Valley Farm, has been in the care of the National Trust since 1943 and was leased to the Field Studies Council about a year later. A wide range of residential field-study courses, available to all, is run from the

centre, although the properties are not open to the casual visitor –
and there are more than enough of these!

Flatford is now a very busy place, with car-parks, coach parties,
a tea shop, gift shop and museum, and boats for hire adjacent to
the arched wooden bridge. It is not a place for quiet study or
exploration on bank holidays, weekends or almost any time
throughout the summer season. In fact, when I was last there in
March, there were so many visitors that it might have been a
weekend in August, although the hot, sunny day, as well as the
crowds, contributed to this impression.

John Constable was born in 1776 in East Bergholt, just up the
winding lane from the river, was educated in nearby Dedham and
worked for a time for his father at the mill, painting in his spare
moments; and it was painting that drew him to London and the
Royal Academy school in 1800. He devoted himself almost from
the beginning to landscapes, and although some of his subjects
were found in the Lake District and at Salisbury, Brighton and
Hampstead, where he lived during the latter part of his life, it was
the Stour that held him captive: 'The sound of water escaping
from mill-dams, willows, old rotten planks, slimy posts and
brickwork, I love such things,' he wrote.

Stour barges and other craft were often subjects of his paintings
and drawings. Fishing-boats at Manningtree and shipping at
Harwich also featured in his studies. His well-known painting
Boat-building near Flatford Mill, depicting a planked-up Stour
barge, is the scene of the dry dock now restored by the River Stour

Flatford Mill

Trust. Examples of his work are in the Tate Gallery, the National Gallery and the Victoria and Albert Museum in London, and locally at the Minories Gallery in Colchester and at the Christchurch Mansion House, Ipswich.

But the scenes Constable immortalized in his paintings are all about you in the Stour Valley, and although most of the old river mills have gone, the pastoral landscapes with their distant churches remain – and the place-names: Langham, Dedham, Stratford St Mary, Higham, Stoke-by-Nayland, Nayland – villages steeped in the atmosphere of the past, some cresting the wooded slopes, others in the valley itself.

Through the water-meadows from Flatford it is an easy walk to Dedham bridge. Just downsteam of this is Smeeth's boatyard, another centre from which you can explore the river in a hired rowing-boat. Although this small yard is now concerned mainly with the building and maintenance of its dinghy hire fleet, some fine sea-going yachts were at one time built there. Behind the boatyard I found the remains of a motorized Stour lighter with the rusty prop shaft and propeller still intact.

Just beyond the bridge is the mill pool with its pollarded willows leaning over the banks, and towering above the scene, Dedham Mill, which has been converted into a smart apartment block; stretch the imagination and you can visualize the ancient mill with its waterwheel that stood in its place when Constable painted it, for the sluices and lock and the lock cottage have changed little since that time.

Restored dry dock, Flatford

Like many other small towns and villages in the area of the Stour, Dedham was a busy centre when the wool trade was flourishing in the Middle Ages. Dedham's magnificent church dates from the fifteenth century and owes much to the wealthy clothiers. There are some fine examples of Tudor and Georgian architecture in the High Street, and two delightful coaching inns, the Sun Hotel and the Marlborough Head, either of which will satisfy your thirst and appetite. Close to the village is Castle House, in which the late Sir Alfred Munnings, the equestrian artist, lived for many years. The house is open to the public at certain times during the summer season.

Above Dedham Mill the river winds its way through lush water meadows to Stratford St Mary, the riverside path taking you through the tunnel under the A12 bridge at the southern end of the village. Nearby is Le Talbooth, a fine restored seventeenth-century toll-house where dues were collected for the upkeep of the bridge; it is now a well-known restaurant fronting the river, with a landing-stage at the edge of the garden.

Stratford St Mary was an important staging-post for the horse-drawn coaches travelling from London to Norwich, but its history goes back to Roman times, when there was a settlement there. The village suffered from the increasing A12 traffic until the mid 1970s, when the bypass was built, a consoling development for the residents and, fortunately, one that has not spoiled the valley, since its low level hardly intrudes on the views from downstream until you are nearing the bridge. And from the north side of the river it is concealed by trees and the village itself. The main street is a pretty stretch where the tree-lined river flows alongside it, so close that you could dip your toe into the water from the road verge, and the only blot is the tall block of the pumping-station at the northern end. The lock gates, almost opposite the Swan, one of four old inns, can be crossed, leading on to a choice of footpaths on the other side.

All this area is a paradise for the rambler; the whole length of the valley and its surrounding countryside is criss-crossed with footpaths, and a local guide is essential. Apart from the Ordnance Survey Pathfinder series, I have found the most useful guides are the footpath maps compiled and published by Wilfred George of Aldeburgh. The series covers many areas of Suffolk, including Constable Country, and can be bought for a few pence from souvenir and bookshops and tourist offices in the regions concerned.

From Stratford you might move on to Langham in Essex, whose church, high on the hillside overlooking the valley, provided the view for Constable's *Dedham Vale*; or you might take the northern side of the river to the little village of Higham, with its triangular green and timbered houses. A tributary of the Stour, the Brett flows under Higham bridge at the bottom of the hill and joins the Stour close to the church.

Higham is the location of the first of the season's point-to-point races which take place in February each year. It was the first meeting I attended, back in the distant past, but whenever I am in the area and see the announcement posters at the end of January it is a pleasant reminder that spring is not far ahead.

A mile along the road from Higham is Thorington Street, a village of one pub and a few houses and Elizabethan Thorington Hall, where the road crosses another tributary, the Box, which winds its narrow course from Boxford to flow into the Stour within a mile of the Brett–Stour confluence. It is well worth taking the riverside lane past the Hall to reap the reward round the first bend in the shape of Thorington Mill, a picturesque white weatherboarded building with its overhanging hoist lift and the placid stream of the Box and mill pool at the rear. The waterwheel has long since gone, but when I was there a notice on the wall announced that stone-ground flour was available, an unexpected

Thorington Mill

revelation that there are rural corners where the fruits of the past are still with us.

From Thorington the road to Stoke-by-Nayland rises to a high ridge; as you approach the rise, turn off to the left into a lane that winds its way down to the Stour at Boxted Mill. Suffolk is a county blessed with pretty, winding lanes that are, fortunately, still quiet byways, and the one in question is no exception. It is no more than half a mile to Boxted Bridge, and the scene is well worth the detour. The lock has gone, but the mill house provides a delightful backdrop to the large mill pool with its surround of trees, cascading weir and the little island crowned with osiers; to complement the picture, just below the bridge are a charming old cottage and a small riverside lawn.

The road along the ridge to Stoke-by-Nayland is one of my favourite stretches. The views on either side and down the valley towards the estuary, with the churches of Dedham and Higham in the distance, are quite superb and contradict the generally held belief that all East Anglia is flat.

On the highest point of the ridge is Stoke-by-Nayland, a small village with a cluster of three inns all within yards of the crossroads, and a fifteenth-century church with a 120-foot tower which is a landmark the compass round. The church contains some fine brasses, including one to Lady Katherine Howard, grandmother of Anne Boleyn and Katherine Howard, wives of the womanizing King Henry VIII. Like the other churches in the Stour Valley, it is well known for its associations with Constable. The view from the tower would have been just as dramatic to him as it is today, except that now in clear weather you can see the cranes of Felixstowe, twenty miles away.

From the crossroads, the route to the south-west takes you downhill and across the bed of the valley to join the Stour again at Nayland, another medieval village that owes much of its fine architecture to the wealth generated by the cloth-making industry. The narrow streets are avenues of properties of varying periods, with many timber-framed houses and overhanging upper storeys to catch the eye.

The Anchor Inn, on the bank just below the bridge, provides a riverside car-park and garden, and there is a landing-stage here built by the River Stour Trust. The church dates from around 1400 and has many historical features. The altar-piece is a painting by Constable of *Christ Blessing the Bread and Wine*, one of three ecclesiastical subjects he painted. (The other two also hung in churches: one at Manningtree, which was removed to Feering, and another in St Michael's Church at Brantham, which is now on loan to Ipswich Museums and Galleries.)

Upstream of Nayland the river passes under the Colchester–Sudbury road to Wissington Mill, Wormingford, Bures and Sudbury; the winding waterside banks and wooded slopes remain a lush slice of country to explore, although the Nayland area is the westerly boundary of what is generally referred to as Constable Country, and I find it is Dedham Vale and the estuary beyond which draw one inexorably back to the broad, open vista of valley and sky.

There is a choice of routes to take you there: on the Essex side of the river through Boxted and Langham to Stratford St Mary, or the lane from the crossroads at Stoke-by-Nayland through Witham Marsh and Raydon to the Hadleigh–Bergholt road (B1070) which runs under the A12 to return you to Constable's birthplace.

The house in East Bergholt in which Constable lived as a boy has gone, although a clue to its location remains in the stable block and railings. The handsome Tudor church is unusual in that it presents an unfinished tower, with the bells in a timbered cage in the churchyard. One local legend tells that each time the tower was built, the Devil knocked it down; another suggests that Cardinal Wolsey promised to finance it but fell from grace before he could do so; another reason could have been the decline in the cloth trade. Whatever the cause, the bells have always been rung in the cage, and this has not detracted from their fine peal.

From East Bergholt it is a short run downhill to Brantham and on to the north bank of the estuary. The route following the river to Shotley peels off the Manningtree–Ipswich road (A137) on the outskirts of Brantham at the Bull Inn. The road is narrow, undulating, twisting through villages and cornfields with panoramic views of the Stour estuary. For most of its way it is no more than a quiet country lane, giving access to numerous footpaths and a host of other lanes that criss-cross the Shotley peninsula.

Some interesting properties come to hand before Stutton village is reached. Stutton Mill House, nestling in the eastern corner of Seafield Bay and looking up the estuary towards Manningtree and Cattawade, has an enviable location. The mill has gone, and the site and mill stream now form the delightful gardens of the house, which is a private residence. Canada geese, ducks and a pair or two of swans in the grounds and on the saltings just outside the sluice seem to have claimed the territory as their own. A long private road leads down to the house, but there is footpath access to the shore, and the area can also be reached along the sea-wall via the Bull Lane footpath off the main road between Brantham railway bridge and the Bull.

One or two fine period houses occupy the wooded slopes nearing Stutton Ness, the point which forms the westerly tip of Holbrook Bay. Stutton Hall is Elizabethan, with an unusual gateway in the brick wall which surrounds the gardens; Crowe Hall, a neighbouring house downstream, was built in the same period but transformed into the Gothic style during the last century, with turret and battlements that can be seen from the river. Through the village and close by the church is Stutton House, formerly the rectory, and down the adjacent footpath is a glorious view in spring across a field of daffodils to the sloping greens of the Royal Hospital School at Holbrook. The school, for the sons of officers and men of the Royal and Merchant Navies, was transferred from Greenwich in 1933 and was opened by the future King Edward VIII, then Prince of Wales. The building is an impressive sight from the footpath and the river, with its tall clocktower central to the two neat arms of the main block; at the rear, staff houses either side of the Holbrook road form a village of their own. The most attractive spot in Holbrook is the old mill and stream, but to .the thirsty rambler the local pub, the Compasses, might be an equal draw.

There are numerous water-walks hereabout, including those around Alton reservoir nearby and Holbrook Creek. The creek can be reached either from Stutton church along the boundary of the school grounds or via the track from Lower Holbrook. At low water the creek dries out, revealing a vast expanse of mudflats filling Holbrook Bay as far as the deep-water channel flanking Wrabness shore directly opposite. The creek is a placid little haven with a number of moorings for small boats which take the mud after each tide, and was the home port of the steamer *Puffin*.

I never revisit the creek without thinking of *Puffin*, for I sailed in

Royal Hospital School, Holbrook

Holbrook Creek

her on many occasions when Bob Partis was her owner. An ex-marine engineer in steam, Bob Partis has been a steamboat enthusiast for most of his life and had lovingly restored the little ship over the years. A toot on the whistle and a puff of smoke were the familiar salutation he brought to the finishing-line of east-coast barge and smack races when *Puffin* was working as a committee boat. And he was apt to blow the whistle on other occasions, too! Not that he needed to draw attention to his traditional little ship from the Steam Age midst the slim plastic hulls of racing yachts and diesel-driven power craft during the East Anglian sailing season, for the sight of her black hull and slender smokestack puffing through the fleet was sufficient to have every pair of eyes focused on her.

Puffin was a teak fifty-two-foot Naval Harbour Service launch built in 1919. Under the tender care of her skipper her machinery purred sweetly, pushing her thirty-one tons along at a steady nine knots and burning a hundredweight of coal per hour in the process. She was a spacious craft, with five berths, a workmanlike wheel-house and a roomy saloon and galley aft. The boiler and engine took up the bulk of her midship section, but there was space enough below and above decks for the enthusiastic party the skipper generally had on board. The party usually included Wally Angel, another 'steam' man and ex-marine engineer, and I can recall times when he and I shared the duty of feeding the firebox or watched from the deck the fleet of old-timers as they rounded the race buoy. I felt with a tinge of pride that I was actively associated, albeit temporarily, with a past tradition that was well worth keeping alive, along with the east-coast sailing-barge and fishing-smack.

Up on the ridge another half-mile downstream, the little village of Harkstead can be seen from the river, with footpaths running down to the shore. A pleasant beach follows the bank of the river round Harkstead Point as far as the saltings just west of Erwarton Ness. This is the last point on the Suffolk bank before reaching the harbour and provides splendid views of Parkeston Quay just down river on the other side, and the long curve of Erwarton Bay to the jetties and boats off Shotley Gate.

Erwarton is a favourite anchorage for those sailors who visit the Queen's Head. The channel is close inshore, a few yards off the old barge quay, whose timbered stumps still stand solidly upright

The steamboat Puffin

across the beach to join the wagon track over the bank. The Ness has been farmed for several generations by the Wrinch family, who at one time owned a fleet of five or six 'stackies'. Their barges and horse-drawn wagons were a familiar sight at the quayside when loading hay or straw or other farm produce and returning with agricultural supplies, including London 'muck' – but not, of course, as a mixed cargo! Many of the waterside farmers owned their own fleets when the barge traffic was at its height, and the remains of their small quays along the estuaries and in the creeks of East Anglia are a constant reminder of the trade.

There is little to attract the visitor in Shotley Street village but Shotley Gate at the end of the peninsula brings you down to the Stour again, with Parkeston Quay just across the water, and Harwich town and harbour at the confluence of the two estuaries, where there is always something of interest going on.

HMS *Ganges*, the naval training establishment, was the focal point of Shotley Gate, and the village grew up adjacent to it. Opened in 1907, it took its name from the training ship that was berthed at Shotley in 1898. The ship was removed to Chatham when the base was commissioned ashore, and until 1976, when it was closed, the boys were a familiar sight in the village and out on the river practising their seamanship in cutters and whalers. The buildings still dominate the area, but many of them have been temporarily converted to other uses.

The company that took over the 150-acre site have recently opened the Shotley Point marina, with entrance lock, restaurants,

Old barge quay, The Ness, Erwarton

bar, supermarket and a host of other facilities serving the boat-owner; further plans include a residential development and a number of holiday homes overlooking the yacht basin. The famous 142-foot mast, which was manned by the boys on ceremonial occasions, has been restored and is back in its old position on the parade ground, a listed landmark that will remain as a reminder of HMS *Ganges* when the old buildings have gone.

For some reason the Stour has never been popular with the yachtsman, although with permanent moorings at Wrabness, in Holbrook Creek and at Manningtree, more pleasure craft are to be seen today than in the past. The broad mudflats hem in the narrowing channel, particularly above Wrabness, and there are no tantalizing bends in its banks to reveal a change of scene as there are on the Orwell. It is wide open to the westerlies for most of its ten miles to Manningtree, but the shorelines with their wooded slopes are no less beautiful than its neighbour's.

It has always been a fascinating river to me, maybe because it was the first estuary I sailed on, as far back as I can remember, and because it is still a quiet, almost deserted waterway when compared with most of the others. Of course, with the quayside improvements at Mistley and the dredging of the channel the freight traffic is increasing; but when I sailed up recently with Cy Blackwell, who runs the P & Q Sailing Centre at Woolverstone, there was no other craft under way. Admittedly, it was March, before the sailing season began; and if most of the wintering wildfowl had gone, there were still the estuary birds and waders – dunlin, redshanks, oystercatchers, curlews – edging back with the tide as it filled the gullies and lapped the saltings. In the shallows close to Holbrook creek was the still, sentinel figure of a heron seeking his catch; out in the channel the unusual appearance on the river of a red-throated diver, undisturbed by our passage, and all the way upstream the cormorant was a frequent shadow of flight across our bows.

For the most part the estuary scene has changed little over the years, except for the buoyage system. New, brightly painted buoys and beacons now mark the channel right up to Mistley. I remember the channel and shoal marks when they were no more than half-submerged logs like tarred railway sleepers that were almost as difficult to find as the shoals themselves. But perhaps a more succinct way to sum up the position as it used to be for the sailor is to refer to the comment quoted in Hervey Benham's well-known book on the east-coast sailing-barges, *Down Tops'l*: 'You can't see the buoys in the Stour unless there happens to be a cormorant sitting on them.'

ORWELL BRIDGE

Stanley Bennet

3

The Commercial Tideway

The sailor has always been able to see the buoys on the Orwell with or without the aid of the cormorant – at least from about the end of the last century, when the more prominent, coloured metal buoys were introduced, the forerunners of those we see today.

For centuries the Orwell estuary has been an important commercial tideway. Its history, and that of Ipswich at its head, goes back to the Romans who settled there, establishing a trading-post and thus creating the early beginnings of the port. It grew in the Saxon era, suffered under the plundering Danes and in 1016 saw the arrival of Canute, whose armies swept to London, where he was eventually proclaimed king of England. A century or so before King Alfred's navy had fought off the invading Norsemen where the long shoal of Shotley Spit runs into Harwich harbour, and a reminder of the battle may be found in the more dramatic name 'Bloody Point' by which the spit has always been known.

The invasions of today are of the commercial and pleasure variety, less blood-curdling but not without potential damage to the river and its environment. The development of the area in recent years has brought a rapid increase in its importance as a trade route, and traffic has not yet reached its peak; further expansion is under way at Ipswich and the port of Felixstowe, the latter creeping further up river.

Apart from the considerable increase in traffic – commercial and pleasure – the changes that have taken place since I first sailed on the river have affected only certain parts, mainly at the entrance, with the Felixstowe port extensions and the marina at Shotley Point, and at the approaches to Ipswich. For most of the way along its nine-mile course the shorelines – except for the Levington and Woolverstone marinas – remain, along with the wooded banks and rising countryside, just as I remember them.

In the changing agricultural climate of today, when farmers are encouraged to release land for alternative development, the potential threat to the rural and wildlife scene is obvious. Some farmers who have neglected to preserve their own natural environment (the destruction of wildlife habitats with the rooting-out of hedges and filling of ditches to increase production now no longer essential) might well be tempted by the developer's offers. On the other hand, the new scheme promoted in the eastern counties by the Countryside Commission to provide extra grants to farmers who are prepared to improve or create wildlife habitats on land set aside from agricultural production, should reduce such threats, encourage the restoration of areas damaged by intensive farming and significantly increase the conservation of the countryside and its wildlife.

Of course, many farmers along with the old estate-owners are

Barge match, River Orwell

as conscious of the need for conservation as are the protective societies and trusts. Their co-operation with these bodies, together with the councils concerned, has resulted in so much of our estuary and coastal surroundings being designated Areas of Outstanding Natural Beauty, thus ensuring they remain so. The Orwell can still lay claim to such qualities. For most of the way every turn in the river portrays it, the scenes on shore confirm it.

Take the by-road to Shotley church, for instance. This narrow, undulating lane, a turning off the Shotley road (the main route along the peninsula from Ipswich to Shotley Gate), takes you to the old village, nestling on a hill which rises from the marshes with a grand view down the lower estuary to the harbour and the sea – a lonely, peaceful place with a few old cottages dominated by a church of strange design:

> Shotley Church without a steeple.
> Drunken parson, wicked people.

This old adage probably originated in the days when smuggling was rife along the East Anglian coast and in the estuaries and the villages bordering them. In the eighteenth and early nineteenth centuries smuggling was a well-organized business, and the Revenue men had a dangerous, unenviable task arresting the culprits and finding the cargoes they brought ashore. Any temporary hide for the illicit gin, brandy, lace and silks brought in by the 'free traders' (a term used by those involved that might have given a more legitimate ring to their business), was found to defeat the eye of the Revenue; some goods were buried ashore, others sunk in containers underwater to be retrieved when the coast was clear; yet others were hidden in farm buildings, cellars, even churches, particularly those in the care of a parson who might be partial to a tipple!

If there was ever any truth in the couplet, it is not taken literally today, except in the description of the church, whose roof-line is not even broken by a tower. In fact, from the river it must often be mistaken for a farm building. But if the church is unusual, so is the churchyard, for in this serene and isolated spot many British and German sailors are buried, a fitting resting-place overlooking the river for those who died at sea during the war.

From the church a bridleway takes you downhill and eventually onto the sea wall at Collimer Point and a riverside walk upstream to Pin Mill. A less arduous way to get to this pretty waterside hamlet is via the lane from Chelmondiston village on the Shotley–Ipswich road, which ends at the river. It meanders down, clinging to the side of a little valley now sadly cluttered with small modern houses; but where the river springs into view, old terraced cottages, boatsheds, chandlers, boats and barges sweep you back into yesterday's world. The end of the lane joins the long hard that runs almost to the deep-water channel. The river here is now a very crowded anchorage, with yachts moored on either side of the channel, stretching upstream and downstream all within a stone's throw of passing freighters. On shore, adjoining the hard and a welcome sight to sailors and other thirsty travellers, is the Butt & Oyster, a grand old inn in the traditional style that has been a favourite hostelry with sailing-barge skippers and east-coast yachtsmen for generations. The high tides lap its base walls, and you could take a pint through the bar window whilst still in your dinghy.

At any time of the year there is always a shapely sailing-barge or two sitting on the hard, but a few of the old hulls have been turned into houseboats, some of which have seen better days, although these are moored inshore just downstream of the pub, practically concealed by the overhanging cliff-side trees. Fortunately, the cliff-top plantation is now protected by the National Trust and immune from despoliation, although, of course, it suffered in the storm of '87.

The Butt & Oyster, Pin Mill

Raybel *on Pin Mill hard*

Pin Mill has always been a centre for barge folk and sailors. It was for many years the home of Bob Roberts, perhaps the best-known barge skipper of all. He wrote two fascinating books, *The Last of the Sailormen* and *A Slice of Suffolk*, the latter being an endearing account of the Suffolk coast but with the emphasis on Pin Mill, the river and its characters. The first title is appropriate enough, for he *was* the last. As master of the *Cambria* he continued to trade under sail until the 1960s. Writing the final paragraphs of his book in the *Cambria*'s cabin while the mate at the wheel headed her seaward outward bound from the London river to Yarmouth with a cargo of bran, Bob Roberts concludes:

Her bowsprit down and two jibs set, all her canvas is drawing to a freshening westerly breeze and the smooth water chatters by as she makes a comfortable seven knots. Coming down London River a big Gravesend tug gives us a cock-a-doodle-doo on his whistle and I daresay the old barge justified the compliment as she heeled to the breeze, her gilt scrolls and varnished spars bright in the mid-day sun.

The last of the sailormen, indeed, but not yet, not quite yet, a thing of the past.

How right he was! Although the cargoes have gone, the Thames barge sails on. Now, thirty years later, more than fifty of these handsome old craft, with their great spread of canvas, lovingly restored by owners, skippers and crews, continue to enhance the east coast and its estuaries, no longer trading, just sailing and cruising – and racing.

There are a number of barge matches each year; probably the most famous starts and finishes at Pin Mill, organized by the Pin Mill Sailing Club with headquarters just upstream of the hard. The event, in June, which brings so many of these old-timers together, is a memorable one, drawing an audience to every vantage-point on land and aboard a miscellany of craft afloat. Forget the powerboats, the container ships, the cars and those little modern houses ashore, and for a little while at such a time you are back at the turn of the century.

But Pin Mill was a bustling centre long before that. It offered a workers' base close to Butterman's Bay, just downstream, where sailing-ships from the Continent and elsewhere, too large to proceed to Ipswich, discharged their cargoes into barges which lightered them up the final reaches to the port. At one time, dredging-smacks, similar to the old fishing-smacks you can still see today, sailed from Pin Mill to the West Rocks off Harwich to dredge for septaria, a clay which set so hard that it was called 'Roman cement stone'; it was used in the building of coastal fortifications, including those at Harwich, and a thriving export trade was developed.

Pin Mill is still a very pretty place, and like all pretty places it tends to get swamped with visitors during the season. To escape the crush, make your way along the beach over the Grindle (a little stream), past Harry King's boatyard and the sailing club, onto the path that follows the river upstream to Woolverstone Park. This is one of the most delightful walks on the banks of the Orwell, with sloping arable fields on one side, the saltings on the other and the trees of the park ahead. Within the boundary of the park near the water's edge is the well-kept lawn of the Royal Harwich Yacht Club, providing a broad view from the windows of the lounge-bar down river and across to Orwell Park on the Nacton shore, with a variety of sailing-craft on the mooring trots either side of the channel.

On the bluff the other side of the club is a picturesque little Gothic cottage, the Cathouse, so called because of its legendary link with smuggling days, when a white cat was placed in the window on dark nights, a signal to the smugglers that the area was clear of the Revenue and they could safely land their cargoes.

The cottage has been restored in recent times, and it is good to see that the owners continue the cat tradition.

A private road runs through the park from the main road serving the club and the large marina just downstream of it. Woolverstone Hall, in the centre of the park, built in 1777 for the Berners family, was for many years a boarding school of the old GLC. The school was recently closed and the Hall and grounds put on the market. One wonders what its new role will be.

Footpaths criss-cross the park, one leading through to Freston, a park of equal beauty, with oaks and copper beeches overlooking grazing-meadows that run down to the beach. From the shore and the river you have the best views of Freston Tower, the Tudor folly that stands six storeys high on the rising ground. It was built for the de Freston family in the sixteenth century. There is more than one tale to describe its purpose. One suggests it was a watchtower, a look-out for ships coming up the estuary; another explains it as a study centre for de Freston's daughter, each room one above the other, used for a different subject in the day's curriculum, ending up, after an afternoon break, with astronomy on the top floor. What this did for her education is not known.

From Freston Park you come down onto the Strand, where the Shotley–Ipswich road curves alongside the river and under the

River Orwell from Pin Mill

Freston Tower

Orwell bridge. The bridge is over 140 feet high, but the largest of the ships – the two 10,000-ton North Sea ferries providing a twice-daily service between Ipswich and Rotterdam (Europoort) – only just have sufficient clearance at mast height at high tide. Where the river curves into the heart of the docks, the inlet to the left is Ostrich Creek, and crossing it is Bourne Bridge, which carries the road into the town. Fox's Marina on one side of the creek is the base for the East Coast Boat Show, which takes place each year in early summer, and on the other side is the Orwell Yacht Club.

The port of Ipswich has had a chequered history from the time it was the first primitive settlement of the Romans. Trade prospered and declined through the early hostile centuries, but by the fifteenth century, when a longer period of stability prevailed, it grew in size and in trade and was nominated the fourth most prosperous port in the country, handling a variety of cargoes to and from the Continent; but over the next 200 years trade was on the decline again through the increasing piracy of the French and the wars with the Dutch; another disaster was the silting-up of the river.

All these impediments led to the creation of a flourishing shipbuilding industry early in the seventeenth-century, which in turn encouraged improvements in the river. The improvements were not maintained, however, even though a canal was dug along the River Gipping to Stowmarket. It was opened in 1798 but was hardly used

Ipswich docks

and soon fell into decline, while the silt around the quays was threatening to kill the port off altogether. Finally the local merchants got together, and in 1805 their activities resulted in the appointment of the river commissioners whose duties included 'deepening, widening, cleansing and otherwise improving the river'. With the revival of trade and with the dues on goods and shipping, the commissioners were able to propose the building of an enclosed dock on the north bank. It was opened in January 1842 and was for a number of years the largest enclosed dock in the country.

An interesting feature on the north bank is the Old Custom House, built in 1845 and still serving an important function as the headquarters of the Ipswich Port Authority. It was designed by a young architect, J.M. Clark, who also designed St John's Church in Woodbridge. Although its balconies, balustrades and columns represent another example of the rather grandiose style favoured by architects in the Victorian era, its façade does present a certain authoritative character synonymous with its lawful purpose.

A less significant building of the period still in use is the old lock-keeper's house on the west side, at the side of the original entrance to the dock. By 1877 the expansion of trade beyond the Continent required further improvements in facilities, which included a new lock entrance at the southern end in direct line with the river channel. This was opened in 1881 and the original entrance closed off; but the lock-keeper's house remained and is now, and has been for many years, the harbour master's office. The expansion during the past few years, down river of the wet dock, appears to have visually isolated the office from much of the action; but this does not affect the duties the increasing traffic dictates. Recent years have seen the fastest growth in the port's history, and it is still expanding, handling trade from many parts of the world.

The advent of the ro-ro ferry, the bulk carrier and the container ship has brought about a decline in general cargo, and to accommodate the modern handling systems quays have been built at the West Bank Terminal and new berths provided on the opposite side at Cliff Quay. Future developments downstream include extension of the West Bank complex towards Ostrich Creek and a ro-ro terminal at the end of Cliff Quay. This river frontage of present operations and future development is dominated by the old power station (no longer operating) behind it; how long the structure will remain is anyone's guess.

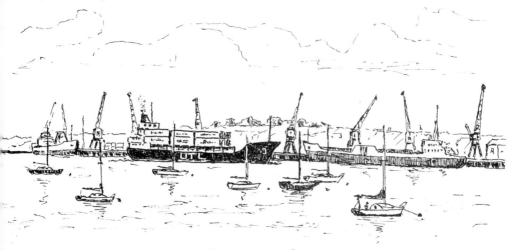

Cliff Quay, Ipswich

With so much of the commercial activity going on down river, trade has moved out of the wet dock and in the main has left it for more leisurely pursuits. It still has a Victorian atmosphere about it, with some of the old wharfs and warehouses now being used for a less industrial purpose. At Wherry Quay, which is a watersport centre, with yachts and sailing-dinghies berthed where sailing-ships and barges once traded – and where you can often see a restored barge or two today, there is a club, restaurants, shops with a nautical theme and quayside pub. It is good to see that most of the changes taking place are in keeping with the old port's character; the old maltings, where the New Cut takes the tidal stream under Stoke Bridge, have been converted into apartments whilst still retaining their original appearance. These residential and leisure developments will, when complete, have all the attraction of a port village in a traditional setting. It is easier to berth a boat here than park a car, but either way it is well worth a visit.

Ipswich is a busy, modern, go-ahead town with a long history, although few features remain to illustrate it except in the museums and galleries. Its past has been much recorded in many books on the region; one that focuses its subject exclusively being *Ipswich – Town on the Orwell* by Robert Malster, a short, well-documented history which is a handy guide when touring the town. But unless you are on the historical trail – or a shopping expedition, I would suggest leaving the crowded streets and taking the old Felixstowe road, following the river down to the quieter shores below Nacton and Levington.

Nacton is a village associated with the name of Margaret Catchpole, the heroine of another romantic affair of the late eighteenth century of which much has been written, including a book by the Revd Richard Cobbold in 1846, which made Margaret's name known far beyond her native village. Cobbold would have known the facts, even though he may have embroidered them a little in his story, for Margaret was employed by the Cobbold family, who grew fond of the girl and made every effort to save her from the consequences of her later misdeeds.

A strong-willed, passionate young woman, Margaret fell in love with Will Laud, a smuggler who was encouraged into the 'free trade' by the notorious John Luff. Her love for Will Laud was demonstrated in her desperate ride to London on a horse stolen from her master's stables when she received a message that Laud was awaiting her there. There was no sign of her lover, and when she sold the horse at Aldgate, she was arrested for stealing the animal – at a time when the sentence for that crime was death. Through the influence of the Cobbold family she was reprieved and the sentence commuted to transportation to Australia. But for some obscure reason she was left to languish in Ipswich gaol, from which she was later assisted in escaping by Laud and John Luff.

The irony of the climax of the tale is that Laud had intended to give up his evil ways, and in the pre-arranged plans of escape he was determined to take his lover to the Netherlands and a new life. A ship was organized to pick them up from a lonely beach at Orfordness. At the appointed time a brig stood offshore at Shingle Street as the three fleeing characters arrived. But the happy ending was not to be. Margaret's gaoler, assisted by the Revenue men, had tracked them to the shore. A fight ensued, Laud and Luff were shot dead on the beach, and Margaret was finally deported to Australia.

The wild, lonely beaches around Shingle Street, and the marshes behind them, remain today much as they were when the smugglers haunted them, and on a moonlit night it is easy to imagine the drama enacted that brought an end to Margaret's romance; but Nacton is still a pretty little village, particularly that end of it that has escaped modern residential development, where quiet lanes and wooded riverside walks conjure up a romantic but less violent picture.

Orwell Park is one showpiece here. A magnificent house with grounds sweeping down to the river, it is now a boys' preparatory school. Towards the close of the Victorian era it was the home of Colonel George Tomline, a wealthy, rather enigmatic but far-sighted gentleman, who established the first dock at Felixstowe from which the present great port has developed. But a century or so before, Orwell Park was the seat of Admiral Vernon, who won fame with the capture of Portobello from the Spanish. The admiral was nicknamed 'Old Grog' from his taste for wearing a grogram coat, a coarse fabric of mohair and wool. In an attempt to improve discipline in the Navy, he introduced a watered-down version of the seamen's rum ration, and thereafter it was always referred to as 'grog'. Incidentally, a further local reminder of the admiral is in the form of a new channel buoy recently laid in the river just off the park shore – it is called 'Grog'.

Orwell Park is adjacent to another fine estate, for just downstream of it is Broke Hall, a noble Gothic mansion with splendid views of the estuary. It was the home of an equally famous admiral, Sir Philip Bowes-Vere Broke, who won more honours when, in command of the *Shannon*, he captured the American frigate *Chesapeake* in a brief and historic fight off Boston in 1813. Broke Hall has now been adapted internally in line with present property trends into self-contained apartments. Not that the changing patterns will alter the landscape, for the parklands of both Orwell Park and Broke Hall have been designated an Area of Outstanding Natural Beauty.

The shady lane between the two parks ends close to the shore and gives access to a path that follows the river down to Levington Creek. This is another delightful route which clings to

Pathway near Levington Creek

the wooded cliff edge, eventually opening up a view down the estuary to the Harwich skyline which, for scenic value, is par with anything on the other bank. From here the choice is onto the sea wall of Levington Creek or into the cosy bar of the Ship Inn – assuming it is 'opening time'. The Ship, maintaining all the attractions of its old character, stands next to the church on the fringe of this pretty village, and one path from the river leads to its door.

The lanes hereabout, so close to the estuary, take you back to the main Felixstowe highway, but I find the peaceful influence of the riverbank irresistible, and the wild calls of the shoreline persuade me to join another wooded pathway just downstream of the yacht harbour. Go through the trees at the base of a shallow cliff with the bank sloping to the saltings, and the scene opens out onto a little bay with a sandy beach dissolving into broad mudflats at low tide. Tucked away from the tidal flow, protected by a sea wall, is a fresh-water fishing lake. This unexpected revelation, filling the depression of the little valley inland, turns the bay into an unspoilt haven for wildlife. Two or three small islands in the lake have become the territory of Canada geese and shelduck, which have their larder on the mudflats nextdoor, while other waterfowl have their nests in the verdant fringes of the lakeside. Few places I know, except for the reserves, have a ready-made lagoon adjoining their salt-water feeding-grounds. It must be nice for the fisherman, too.

Out of the bay and up on the cliff of Sleighton Hill, and the lower reach of the estuary is in view; below, the long, curving arm of the sea wall following the river to Fagbury Point, protecting the Trimley Marshes. The rising hinterland conceals the parishes of Trimley St Martin and St Mary, which now join up through the parish of Walton with Felixstowe town. From the Trimley villages bridleways and pathways give access to the river close to Felixstowe Port, but when I was there, some of these were being diverted, others re-routed to accommodate the port's expansion upstream. The multi-million-pound expansion will take the container quays to Fagbury Point, and the important wader and wildfowl habitat of Fagbury mudflats which form an intertidal zone between the point and Fagbury Cliff will be lost under the new development – but not without compensation ...

Freshwater fishing lake with River Orwell in background

Felixstowe Port is a phenomenal twentieth-century success story. Its history is comparatively brief, since it began from the small dock that Colonel Tomline founded which opened in 1886. But it is only in recent years that it has developed into the thriving port it is today. Situated between the old Languard Fort, where the Dutch were repelled in 1667, and Languard Point, now a nature reserve, it has changed the eastern waterfront and skyline

The River Orwell from Trimley

for almost a mile. Its rapid growth over the past twenty-five years
is illustrated by the throughput of cargo and containers from an
annual tonnage of nearly 400,000 tons to over 15 million.

No wonder the traffic has increased in Harwich harbour to
some 24,000 shipping movements annually. It is no place now for
the yachtsman to dally around; he needs to be on the alert and
know where he is going. To help him in this, the Harwich Haven
Authority generously provides a *Yachting Guide to Harwich
Harbour and Its Rivers*. This is issued annually and contains all
the most important information on the harbour and its
approaches, with appropriate directions, regulations and recommended tracks for pleasure craft. It includes a very useful chart,
aerial colour shots and tide tables.

There were no such official guides when I first ventured afloat
there. It was comparatively quiet, and it was easy enough to swing
into the old dock basin to land or pick up a crew member, finding
that one's only company inside was a small coaster or a
sailing-barge alongside Marriage's Mill. The old maltings building
is still there, under the Rank Hovis banner, along with the
singular weatherboarded dock office, and the basin has hardly
changed over the years; it just seems lost in the modern port

developments. Even if you could sail in, you would have difficulty in finding the entrance; but it still remains the terminal for the regular Harwich–Felixstowe ferry, with passenger access through to the public highway.

Out in the harbour, too, in those days, apart from the Continental packets from Parkeston Quay and small freighters and barges *en route* to Ipswich or Mistley, the only excitement was a taxi-ing flying-boat or a low circling seaplane from the air station, which spread itself along the waterfront between the dock and Languard Fort.

The station was established in 1913 and, apart from playing a vital role in the two world wars (the dock came in useful too), it was for many years the home of the Marine Aircraft Experimental Establishment, and a base for testing flying-boats and seaplanes used by the RAF. It remained operational into the early post-war years, its three large hangars in uniform line above the apron and slipways, the huge Titan crane on its concrete pier, a useful landmark, like Harwich church spire, when approaching from the sea. But the flying-boat and seaplane were by that time already in decline, and when they went, the base was used for a while by a helicopter squadron in air/sea rescue which saw the station through to its closure in the later 1950s. The hangars and crane found a renewed life in the expanding port complex, but these too eventually made way for the container terminals.

The old dock, Felixstowe

Today Felixstowe's location, services and trouble-free record continue to invite increasing world-wide trade, demanding yet further expansion. If this were to proceed, there was only one way to go: north, up river over saltmarsh and mudflats to Fagbury Point, to the edge of the Trimley Marshes. It goes without saying

Landguard Point

that this brought a stream of protest from the conservationists, and rightly so. It was not only a further encroachment into an Area of Outstanding Natural Beauty but the loss of a primary estuary environment, particularly the Fagbury mudflats, recognized nationally as part of the Orwell site of Special Scientific Interest for a variety of wading birds. Foremost among the protesters was the Suffolk Wildlife Trust, founded in 1961 and, to quote from the trust's objectives, 'the only charity in the County working for the conservation of all forms of wildlife and the habitats which they depend on'.

The trust's objections, along with the chorus of opposition from national conservancy bodies and supportive MPs, resulted in the Act subjecting the port's expansion to a provision which involved a range of environmental measures to be observed by the dock company. These included the creation of a 208-acre reserve on the Trimley Marshes, the landscaping of the area and the planting of some half-million trees. Altogether, the cost of the measures is running to some £2 million. The cost of setting up the reserve accounts for about a quarter of this, and the port is to contribute sixty per cent of the annual running-costs – up to £15,000 – for the next thirty years. The reserve, which will mark the north boundary of the port's new limits, is being created and managed by the trust.

At the time of writing, work is already in progress on the site, and when completed the reserve will include a mixed habitat of fresh-water lagoons, flooded grasslands and strategically placed hides. The project, welcome though it is in the circumstances, cannot replace the habitat that will be lost, and trust director Derek Moore confirms this.

'The loss of the Fagbury flats is tragic,' he says, 'and can never be replaced, although the nature reserve will have considerable interest in its own right. It must be stressed that species such as the knot, sanderling and grey plover which happily feed on the Fagbury flats will find little to attract them to the fresh-water lagoons of the new reserve.'

Apart from the serious loss of feeding- and breeding-habitats, any large development in a wildlife area on a commercial tideway must add further to pollution. Where development appears unavoidable, strict procedures are now followed to minimize the impact, although the consequences of such developments are likely to go beyond the recovery of any compensating factors.

Fortunately there are no such threats to the wildlife environment four miles or so (as the bird flies) north of Felixstowe, along the quiet shorelines of the Deben …

4

The Deben Shores

After the commercial activity of Harwich harbour and the Orwell, the Deben and its adjoining countryside are certainly a quiet oasis in which to relax and enjoy its unfolding beauty.

There is no commercial traffic on the river now, but no lack of pleasure craft, with numerous yacht moorings grouped in three or four locations on its nine-mile run from Felixstowe ferry, at its entrance, to Woodbridge at the head of the estuary. Here, overlooked by this lovely old market town, are further moorings, boatyards, yacht clubs, a restored tidemill and a yacht harbour – and a typical branch-line railway station adjacent to the quay.

On summer weekends and at the height of the season the river is lit with coloured sails and flashing hulls; but most weekdays and out of season there is little to stir its enticing surface or startle its feeding wildfowl. The Deben has preserved its quiet charm over the years and retains the scenes and sentiments evoked in W.G. Arnott's book *Suffolk Estuary*, which he wrote in 1950. With its

> … wooded banks … sandy beaches and dry landing-places … gently sloping cornfields and lush green marshes, it has no other river to compare with it.
>
> Throughout my life I have spent hours upon it, gazing at the same scenes, watching the eternal round of sowing and harvest and I never tire. Always there is something different, some new vantage-point or setting of the landscape one had not noticed before or some fresh play of the light and shade to bring out the even contours of the skyline. It is a very lovely picture and I want no other for it satisfies me.

George Arnott's view that there is no other river to compare with it would, I know, be shared by most who know it. Unrivalled and unspoilt, its beauty has an essence quieter than that of the Suffolk estuaries just north of it, although these too have a beauty and fascination of their own, creating as they do in many place scenes that evoke a sense of wild isolation.

As on the other Suffolk tideways, the unspoilt qualities of the Deben owe much to the large farming estates along its banks. These landowners have protected the shores and hinterland from any untoward development, and the official conservation designation of such areas further guarantees that the river and adjacent countryside will continue to remain unmolested.

Except in two or three locations there are no public access roads down to the waterside; they run parallel, keeping their distance, with few glimpses of the river, and in nearly all instances, reaching the creeks or sandy beaches means either walking or landing from a dinghy. Even its entrance seems designed by Nature to protect it from intruders, with its shifting shingle bar and fast-running tides.

The relaxation of the river after the tumble of the bar is a welcome relief as you glide past Felixstowe Ferry, which is on the south bank of the entrance; a further relief from the dry throat the exercise might have induced can be found at the Ferryboat Inn.

Felixstowe Ferry is a fascinating little place, with the fishing and boating interests of river and sea. From the waterside it appears to be perched on a great mound of shingle but once in the hamlet you are on level and more common ground. Landing is clean and easy near the ferry jetty, and the boatyard and chandlery are conveniently close at hand. Just south of the entrance two Martello towers, those defence bastions from Napoleonic times, dominate the shoreline, overlooking the approaches from the sea. The hamlet is a residential mixture of old cottages and a few modern houses. Apart from the inn, the sailing club, the boatyard and two or three fishermen's huts, there is a café and a couple of fish stalls, the fresh supplies being brought in daily by the boats moored off the beach amongst the pleasure craft.

The only road to the hamlet is the one from Felixstowe town, the last mile of it winding across the low plateau of the golf course to end at the ferry terminal. Opposite is Bawdsey Quay, the on and off point for passengers, and above it, on the wooded cliff, Bawdsey Manor, occupied by the RAF. It was built for the Quilters in the 1890s and was the family home until 1936, when it was sold to the Air Ministry and became the principal base for the development of radar. The wooded grounds hide the mansion from the ferry, but just south along the beach and from offshore

Fishermen's huts, Felixstowe ferry

the Gothic façade with its cupola-topped towers reveals its striking presence. The manor and the one remaining aerial tower behind it form an unusual landmark from the sea.

The crossing of the river here has been a facility for a long time. It was Sir Cuthbert Quilter who, before the turn of the century, set up a vehicular steam ferry operated on chains. Two of these double-ended vessels were employed, and the service, operated by the Brinkley family, ran until 1931. The present ferry, a motorboat carrying pedestrians only, has been run for many years by Charlie Brinkley, who took over from his father. The ferry link with this well-known local family continues now that Charlie Brinkley shares this duty, and also that of pilot and harbour master, with his son.

From Felixstowe Ferry the sea wall up river offers an easy – and often breezy – walk to Falkenham Creek and beyond. Before reaching the Falkenham Marshes, the wall crosses King's Fleet, so named, it is believed, because in the Middle Ages, when this whole area along the south bank of the river was a great harbour known as Goseford Haven, it was used by the ships of kings. All that remains now is a small creek through the saltings controlled by sluices which link a canal-like waterway running to the fringe of the scattered hamlet of Falkenham. Gradually the land was reclaimed over the years, and now arable fields spread towards the sea wall bounded by dikes, the quiet haunt of swans and other waterfowl.

For a couple of miles upstream from the entrance both shores of the Deben are low and flat, with arable and grazing marshes levelling the eye to distant woods, and it is not until the river winds past Falkenham and Kirton creeks and Ramsholt cliff on the opposite bank that the shorelines suddenly change into the sheltered wooded slopes, shallow cliffs and sandy beaches which contribute so much to its beauty. To pause in a boat here, in the quiet of a closing day, with the pines silhouetted against the sunset glow, the soft chuckle of the tide along the hull, the evening calls of waders, with a pipe to draw on and a drink at hand, is to appreciate to the full the enchantment of the scene.

Even with the chill in the air and that cold out-of-season look, the autumn and winter have their attractions too, with visitors from the north winging in to join wildfowl residents along the deserted river. Kirton Marshes are a winter haunt of brent-geese, and their flight in against a clear, crystal autumn sky is a scene to warm your heart if not your hands. Although the walk from Kirton Creek to the tiny hamlet of Hemley is not best accomplished in wintry weather, it is a sheltered, pretty route in contrast to the exposed sea walls down river. In fact, from the boundary of Kirton Marshes up river, the rambler has a choice of skirting the sea wall and saltmarsh or taking the tree-lined tracks edging arable fields and grazing marshes.

Hemley is the first road access to the river from Felixstowe Ferry, though this is not strictly true, for it peters out into a farm

The River Deben at Hemley

track some distance from the saltmarsh, which is a common feature along this stretch of the Deben. By road from Felixstowe you turn off the A45 for Kirton from where the lane winds through gently undulating country to Newbourn. From the village centre and the pub, the narrow road winds up to join the Hemley–Waldringfield lane. It is certainly a by-lane with its close, overgrown verges, so rural that you would expect to see a pony and trap or a horse-drawn farm wagon rather than a car, and that used to be the scene. The area still has much of the private farming estate appearance about it, the road serving only the few Hemley residents. It ends near the church, which incidentally has a splendid red-brick tower, with a number of cottages, a farmhouse or two and nowhere to leave the car. It is a lovely, remote spot set in essentially walking country.

There are better facilities for car-travellers a mile or so upstream at Waldringfield. A parking-area has been made available in recent years adjoining those of the Maybush Inn and the sailing club, up on the cliff which overlooks the yacht moorings, for this is very much a sailing centre. The channel scours close to the shore at this point; there is a fine stretch of beach occupied mainly by yacht tenders and, in the holiday season, by many visitors.

Waldringfield has developed into a large residential village, its nearness to Ipswich attracting the commuter; but the waterfront has changed little since I first knew it. I remember the inn when it was a small waterman's pub in which to end a rousing day's sailing in convivial company, with hardly room to lift an elbow in the bar. There is now much more space and a wide range of bar food. The gardens, which overlook the quay and boatyard, are a popular place in summer to enjoy a pint whilst watching the activities on the river.

Apart from all the usual services for the yachtsman, the boatyard operates a series of river cruises throughout the season aboard a thirty-eight-foot motorboat with saloon comfort for fifty-four passengers and with the facilities of a bar and on-board meals. A thoughtful welfare feature is that the boat was specially designed to allow access for the disabled and will accommodate up to twelve hospital wheelchair passengers by a system of two hydraulically lifting floor areas. The superstructure on a seagoing hull was designed locally and built in the boatyard. Reg Brown,

The Maybush, Waldringfield

Waldringfield

proprietor of the yard, who has had personal experience of physical disability, wanted to provide an opportunity for the permanently disabled to enjoy the beauties of the river, and this he has achieved with commendable success. He tells me that during the season his cruise passengers include some 4,000 disabled people. For any kind of boating you need to be able-bodied, and it is a pleasant thought that so many of those less fortunate can enjoy a taste of what the Deben sailor can enjoy at any time – getting afloat and exploring the river.

Upstream again and there is Woodbridge. It has long been my favourite town. Although most of its many summer visitors spill into its narrow streets from the bypassing A12 (and some from the railway station), the perfect way to approach it is from the river.

That first glimpse from the last reaches of the estuary reveals in one view the scenic qualities and seafaring associations that contribute so much to its character. The wooded slopes of Kyson Hill running down to the point at Martlesham Creek, the red roofs of the town riding gently above each other topped by the tower of St Mary's, and down on the waterfront Ferry Quay, its boats and boatyards; beyond, the white weatherboarded tidemill, and beyond that the masts of the yachts in the Tide Mill Harbour, which was once the mill pool; few towns can boast such an enticing introduction as does Woodbridge from the river.

It is no surprise to see the narrow streets bustling with summer visitors – and too much traffic – for this small market and seafaring town appears to hold on to all that is worthwhile from the past without giving way to modern developments which have spoiled the character of places elsewhere. Woodbridge has not allowed the commercial trend to interfere too much with its inheritance; nothing has been knocked down that might detract from its character, nothing ugly put up to spoil the beauty of so much of its architecture.

Of course, there have been changes over the years, but little affecting the town centre: residential and some light industry on the outskirts, retirement apartments on the fringe of the town, one of them overlooking the river which I think could have been given a presence more in keeping with its site, although I must admit it did replace an ugly commercial warehouse; a car-park or two, and a road adjacent to the river and the rail line to persuade traffic away from the town centre; but otherwise it holds firmly to its roots. A number of the small inns emphasize the seafaring

Kyson Point

atmosphere one senses in the town, and the Crown Hotel at the head of Quay Street retains much of its character as an old coaching inn.

The town cannot lose sight of its ancient tideway. Quay Street, the northern end of the Thoroughfare, and the rising grounds of Melton Grange Hotel: all reveal glimpses of the river, with the wooded slopes on the other side a backdrop to remind you that such lush country is only a rowboat away.

Woodbridge Harbour

With so many highlights (including a restored tower mill) as well as the tidemill, it is not easy to categorize: all seem essential in making the town what it is. The fine Georgian and Elizabethan houses of Cumberland Street; old shopfronts in the Thoroughfare; Church Street, with a range of early Victorian styles, and at the top St Mary's church and the abbey, a restored Tudor mansion, now occupied by the juniors of Woodbridge School.

The abbey was the family home of the Seckford family, and in this area of the town you cannot go far without being reminded of Thomas Seckford, its wealthy benefactor, who rose to power at the time of Mary I and Elizabeth I. Adjacent to the abbey and the church is Market Hill, its central feature the Dutch-gabled Shire Hall, built by Thomas Seckford in 1575. Over the centuries it has served to house the sessions and been a market for produce and a corn exchange; it is at present used as a court house. Further examples of the endowments of the Seckford Foundation are the old Seckford Hospital, in Seckford Street off Market Hill, and the neat Victorian almshouses nearby, and just outside the town Seckford Hall, said to have been built by Thomas Seckford's father. The mansion, beautifully restored, is now a fine country hotel retaining all the atmosphere of the period with the comforts the traveller expects today.

Another famous Woodbridge figure, but of the more recent past, was Edward FitzGerald, who became a literary celebrity with his translation from the Persian of *The Rubáiyát of Omar Khayyám*. He lived for a time on Market Hill and entertained his friends, among whom was Alfred, Lord Tennyson, at the Bull Inn at the lower end of the square. FitzGerald was an eccentric character who loved the Deben, on which he spent much of his time, particularly aboard a yacht he had built which he called *Scandal*, a name as eye-catching as his eccentric dress, for he was usually seen at the helm in scruffy clothes topped by a stove-pipe hat which, in smart breezes, he managed to retain by means of a scarf fitted over the crown and tied under his chin. Despite his eccentricities or perhaps because of them, he was a much-loved character. He was buried close by the FitzGerald family mausoleum in St Michael's churchyard at Boulge, a pretty hamlet a couple of miles north of the town.

Old houses overlooking the harbour, Woodbridge

Running down past the Bull is New Street, and within a stone's throw of this inn is another, the Bell & Steelyard, a building that at once catches the eye because of the 'yard' overhanging the street. This was a balanced crane with chain slings that lifted a complete wagon before and after it was loaded, a relic to remind you that agriculture and the river trade went hand-in-hand in these East Anglian waterside towns and villages.

One observation of the importance of Woodbridge as a centre of these two trades in the eighteenth-century is recorded by Daniel Defoe in his *Tour Through The Eastern Counties*, published in 1724. He found Woodbridge 'a considerable market for butter and corn to be exported to London'. He described the east Suffolk dairies of that time as 'famous for the best butter, and perhaps the

The Bell & Steelyard, Woodbridge

worst cheese in England'. Defoe obviously enjoyed the taste of local butter, for he went on to emphasize the quality when he wrote: 'I have known a firkin of Suffolk butter sent to the West Indies and brought back to England again, and has been perfectly good and sweet, as at first.' This may have been due in part to the way it was 'barrelled or often pickled in small casks'. He considered Wood-bridge the chief port for the export of Suffolk butter '... which for that reason,' he concluded, 'is full of corn-factors and butter-factors, some of whom are very considerable merchants'. Mer-chants who left the town legacies in the form of some of the fine houses which still remain to be admired.

Another attractive building which emphasizes this eighteenth-century link between farm and sail is the tidemill close to Ferry Quay. I remember talking to an old local millwright, way back in 1948, who a few years before had made a new waterwheel, proudly claiming that he was the only millwright of his generation to have done so, and this was installed in the tidemill at Woodbridge. The mill continued working until the mid 1950s, the last of its kind in the country to do so. It fell into decay when the main oak shaft broke, and it remained derelict over the next ten years or so, when funds were raised to restore it. The whole building was strengthened, the ugly corrugated-iron cladding stripped off and replaced with weatherboarding, a new waterwheel installed and a mill pool created between the river and the yacht harbour. It is open during the season and is a focal-point for artists at any time during the year. The granary next door has for long been an ugly neighbour, but is now in the process of restoration.

The mill overlooks the hard, and from here a ferry has crossed the river to Sutton since ancient times. Boats still operate a service when the tide is right for those visiting Sutton Hoo. This is the site of the Anglo-Saxon burial ship that was excavated in 1939. The wooded slopes from the river rise to the sandy burial ground to which the eighty-nine-foot rowing-galley was hauled nearly 1,400 years ago, leaving archaeologists and historians wondering how such a feat was accomplished. What the excavation of the barrow revealed is well-known recent history. Although none of the ship's timber remained, various metal fastenings were found, and the imprint of her hull in the sandy soil disclosed an accurate picture of her shape and length. Amidships were traces of a wooden chamber thought to have contained the body of an East Anglian king. The wealth of royal possessions found in the ship, believed by the Saxons to ensure a king's life beyond the grave, included silver, gold coins, jewellery, ornamental bowls, a solid gold belt buckle and numerous other priceless artefacts, a treasure trove considered to be the richest 'find' ever discovered in British soil and generously bequeathed to the nation by the owner of the land. They can now be seen in the British Museum.

Although no human remains were found in the great ship, it seems likely that it was the burial-place of King Raedwald, who died around AD 625, a descendant of the great leader Wuffa, who founded the Wauffinga dynasty that had for generations held sway over East Anglia.

A couple of miles or so up river from Sutton Hoo is the charming village of Ufford, a name said to be derived from Wuffa. It nestles around the water meadows of the Deben Valley, russet tile and thatch glimpsed amongst the trees, its timbered and Georgian houses and terraced cottages framed in wooded and flower-decked gardens that scent the lanes and pathways reaching down to the river. The church, dating from 1450, has some fine fifteenth-century bench-ends but is especially noted for its magnificent font cover, eighteen feet high and said to be the most beautiful in the world. It rises in receding tiers of canopied niches terminating in a carved pelican and is a remarkable example of medieval craftsmanship. An ingenious feature of this elaborate cover is that it is telescopic, the lower part sliding up over the superstructure. Fortunately it so impressed the church-wrecker William Dowsing, in 1643, when he arrived to do his work, that the cover was spared, although he did not leave the church unscathed, despite the gallant efforts of the churchwardens, the sexton and the local constable to stop him. Outside the churchyard, near the kissing-gate, the eighteenth-century stocks and whipping-post are further reminders that the village was not always as tranquil as it is now.

The riverside pastoral scenes with their grazing cattle complement this picturesque village, and the water-meadow walks give you another perspective of its delightful setting. Just downstream of the narrow road bridge the river runs through private property, passing the remains of Melton watermill and under the single-track railway bridge. There is no public access between these two points, but you can reach the rail bridge near the tidal limits by walking the river wall up from Woodbridge or Melton or, better still, by taking a dinghy and going up on the tide.

I have never lost my fascination for rivers, particularly tidal rivers, since I first climbed into a boat and began exploring the Stour. There is something about the ebb and flow of the tides, revealing and concealing a strange environment, half-land, half-water, that relieves all tensions. Although in so many places you can observe the results of this natural cycle from the river banks, it can never be as close to you as it is in a boat. On the water you feel part of it, just enough to find your curiosity driving you on. The narrower the waterway, the greater the urge to reach the end of the tide, as if every reed-lined bend will expose the exciting prospect of some new and surprising revelation.

I have known the Deben estuary from its shores and from a boat for long enough, but I had never explored the upper reaches of the river until we took the dinghy on a bright, still morning. When we left the waterfront activity of the town, eventually disappearing between the reedbeds towards the tidal limits, I knew Woodbridge and the adjoining village of Melton would seem a world away. And, of course, they did.

Setting out from the old quay just upstream of the town, the rising tide leisurely covering the sunlit gleam of the mudflats with its rippling sparkle, we took the twisting channel, for there was as yet hardly depth to float the dinghy in the shallows. An hour or so either side of high water the channel is deep enough to take keel boats up to the boatyards at Melton, and on a spring tide even as far as Wilford Bridge, on the eastern fringe of the village, the first road crossing from the river mouth. Opposite the boatyards the old river wall, collapsed in many places, reveals a broad tidal lagoon fronting the Sutton shore, the haunt of Canada geese, shelduck, oystercatcher, swan and heron.

Another half-mile up and the shores close in again to squeeze the river under the low arch of Wilford Bridge. From here the sudden change from an estuary environment to a more pastoral setting is a

Wilford Bridge, looking upstream

marked contrast. A further half-mile and the river is narrowing, twisting, the tall reeds closing in and, with the overhanging trees, concealing the country beyond the banks.

There is little to break the stillness of these upper reaches. The tide is sluggish, gently stirring the weed, the only sounds the rustle of hidden waterfowl in the reeds, the plop of a rising fish. In such a world the outboard motor was a monstrous intrusion, but over a two-mile course from the town it was the only means of reaching our set limits and beating the turn of the tide. Even that was in doubt, for the further we penetrated, the thicker the weed, and every few minutes we were upping the motor shaft to spin the green stuff off the propeller; but in the end we got there ...

Capping the final bend of our course, emphasizing the meditative atmosphere of the river scenery, a peeping glimpse of the tower top of Old Melton church above the reeds and impenetrable bankside foliage. It stands alone, small, isolated and long since redundant, overlooking the meadows, nearly a mile from the village and marking our turning-point.

Going back with the ebb, we felt in harmony. The motor silent, the boat drifting, with now and then a quiet pull on the oars, the

Old Melton church from the Deben

Wilford Bridge, looking downstream

shady foliage of the bank caressing the reeds, the sun bouncing diamonds of light off the placid surface ... so relaxed that we seemed to merge with the surroundings.

I suspect that few sailors who keep their boats at Woodbridge or Melton, and even fewer visitors, are inclined to explore the river above their harbour berths, unless they are of the kind the boating faternity call 'ditch-crawlers'. But the effort in the dinghy is well rewarded. There are no landing-places in the higher reaches, but when the tide serves, you can get ashore at Wilford Bridge and a little further up on the east bank, near the pretty village of Bromeswell. Here, just across the lane from the river, is a small but interesting nature reserve managed by the Suffolk Wildlife Trust, and on the further side of the village, a fish farm where, if you fancy it, you can get a fresh trout for your supper.

The first road access to the estuary downstream on the east bank from Wilford Bridge is at Ramsholt. This is reached via the Sutton–Shottisham road, and at the junction with the Hollesley road at the beginning of Sutton Common there is an easy fieldside walk to the ancient burial ground at Sutton Hoo. In fact, this is the most comfortable route to the site, since it is all on the level and saves the climb to the ridge from the river.

Here you are in the midst of the Suffolk Sandlings, so named because of the light and sandy soil. The Sandlings are great stretches of heathland, coloured in season with gorse, broom, bracken and heather, that spread over so much of the area between the A12 and the coast from Ipswich and Woodbridge to Southwold in the northern part of the county. This land, developed by the earliest farmers, continued for centuries to support grazing stock – cattle, goats and especially sheep; a link with the sheep and the roaming shepherds of these times is acknowledged by such place-names as Sheep Drift Lane, Sutton Walks and Alderton Walks.

More recently much of the heathland has disappeared under the plough. It is poor land for barley and wheat but some root crops thrive in it, particularly carrots. In the last century, when horses were the motive power on farms and elsewhere, carrots were the main ingredient of their daily diet, and the carrot-growers of the Sandlings sent so many barge loads to London for the capital's dray horses that Suffolk became known as 'the carrot county'. Carrots continue to cover a large acreage on these light soils today.

The Forestry Commission is much in evidence, too, managing plantations of Scots pine, the two major areas being Rendlesham and Tunstall forests, which suffered disastrously in the great storm of October '87. It is splendid walking and picnicking country, but it is also country where no one plays with matches or carelessly throws a lighted cigarette end; the results could be catastrophic.

Nowhere in the Sandlings are you very far from an estuary or the sea; in fact, it is the nearness of these physical features anywhere in east Suffolk that make this part of the county so attractive. Along the Sutton road and near the village there are fair walks across estate land to the Deben and again near Shottisham village. From here along a narrow lane it is but two miles to Ramsholt.

There is no village as such at Ramsholt, only a farmhouse, one or two cottages, a fine pub nestling under the brow of the verdant cliff, and the river, strung with moored yachts in summer. It is essentially a sailors' base, and George Collins is the helpful harbour master. For a long time the name of Collins has been well known to yachtsmen here, George succeeding his late father, who was still a very active and familiar figure in the role right up until he died at the age of eighty a few years ago.

Ramsholt

Below the red crag of the hill the old barge quay is well maintained and well used by yachtsmen. Ramsholt Dock, as it is still known, at one time served a small fishing fleet as well as barges, and an old oyster fishery abandoned early in this century has recently been revived. An inviting stretch of sandy beach ends at the river-wall, along which there is a walk upstream to another little beach. The channel is close in here and, because of its rocky (septaria) bottom at this point, is appropriately named 'The Rocks'. It is a favourite anchorage and a delightful spot for a laze or a swim.

Ramsholt church adds another picturesque touch to the riverside scene. Its lonely position on a hill overlooking the river makes it a distinctive landmark, but its most interesting feature is the unusual oval tower, said to date from the thirteenth-century and built originally as a watchtower or beacon to which the church was added a century later.

Ramsholt church

You get the feeling at Ramsholt that you are very much in estate country, and indeed you are, for private land runs all along the east bank of the river and there is no other public road access until you get down to the mouth at Bawdsey. The short route down from Ramsholt is by boat; but it is a pretty drive through winding lanes (watch out for pheasants) through the quiet village of Alderton, with its distant views of the sea, and the adjoining village of Bawdsey which lies a mile or so away from Bawdsey Quay. Across the extensive grounds of Bawdsey Manor, on your approach to the river, the glimpses you catch of the ground-to-air missiles on the cliff remind you that it is still very much an air-defence establishment, although this is scheduled to close in the spring of 1991.

The river front at Bawdsey is a popular place in summer. Here again the channel runs close in to the shore, offering a grandstand view of the movement of craft in and out of the river as well as activities aboard the variety of boats moored off Felixstowe Ferry.

View from the Ramsholt church

But space is limited; it was never a location to take the influx of traffic it often sees during the season, and the short stretch of beach below the road is usually well occupied.

Although there is access to the quay and the beach seaward of it, the area comes under the control of the Ministry of Defence, and a notice warns that you are there are your own risk. The RAF inevitably dominates the waterfront, the boundary of the station flanking the road to the quay which is opposite the main entrance to the manor. There are parking-slots on the quay, and when these have filled, cars squeeze onto the roadside verge just above the beach. To relieve the congestion a picnic- and parking-area has been created amongst the trees where the Bawdsey road turns on the waterfront; but it seems to have made little difference. People tend to use their cars as viewing-stands, and since the new car-park is screened from the river by the trees, the traffic on the road is much the same as it ever was.

For those who prefer to take the air rather than sit in the car, the riverside rambler is a bit hemmed-in here. The beach below the road folds into the saltings a few hundred yards upstream, and the river wall skirting this intertidal zone, protecting the Bawdsey and Ramsholt marshes, is on private land; towards the end of the beach seaward of the quay the tides scour out the steep-to shingle, in places almost to the sea defences of the manor boundary. As these conditions change at intervals, it is advisable to remember the notice on the quay should you stray that far. Not many people do. Needless to say, the shore end on the Bawdsey bank is an isolated place; but there is nowhere better to appreciate the natural barrier protecting the entrance to the quiet haven of the river.

Trudging the narrow, deserted beach in the high wind of an autumn day as the ebb races out of the river to meet the coastal stream is well worth the close vantage-point you have of the boisterous seascape. The emerging banks, the knolls, linking their way seaward, form a huge breakwater on which the moving swells rear up, their tops surfing, to smash themselves on the hard shingle. Somewhere out there midst the white breaking shoal water is the channel over the bar, but the bar buoys are lost in the spume. It is an awesome but thrilling picture, a sort of grand crescendo to the muted tones of the river inland.

More than once I remember being alone, high on the beach above the edge of the turbulent waters, the wind, sharp, moisture-laden, leaving its salty taste on the lips, a lone gull screaming to a lowering sky, the distant roar of the breakers, the near, rasping voice of the shingle; the loneliest of places where river meets the sea in its wilder mood.

For me, all part of the magic of the estuaries.

5

The Magic of the Estuaries

As we approached the north-east tip of the island, the first object to draw our attention on the grass-covered river wall was the notice.

HAVERGATE ISLAND
NO LANDING PLEASE

Following the low-lying eastern shore another mile down river to our landing-point and nosing the boat into the sloping shingle beach, there is another notice with the same request, adding that the island is owned and administered by the Royal Society for the Protection of Birds and is a National Nature Reserve.

However, we were in the warden's boat, and landing was the object of the exercise. John Partridge had welcomed us aboard at Orford Quay on one of those early summer mornings when the haze over marsh and sea precedes the heat of the day, and less than a half-hour later we were stepping ashore near the southern end of the island.

There is something especially fascinating about islands; near or far, small or large, the surrounding waters enhance their isolation and revive that feeling for adventure inherent in boyhood expeditions. The smaller, the more remote the island, the better, and if it is uninhabited, the greater that feeling of the unknown as you implant your footprint in the sand. I have known this kind of immature anticipation in the Orkneys and Shetlands when researching wildlife material for both features and fiction.

Of course, it is not quite like that at Havergate, even though the only inhabitants are the birds and the only humans are the temporary residents in the form of the warden and his assistants who manage the island to protect them. For Havergate is in the River Ore, a couple of miles up from the entrance which is some five miles north along the coast from the Deben.

The island certainly feels remote when you are on it, although all the mod cons of everyday living are not very far away. From the hides overlooking the lagoons on the west side, the shallow heights of Gedgrave with its farmhouse and cluster of cottages rise up beyond the marshes; to the north, the castle keep and the church at Orford stand out above the roofs of the village; yachts and the occasional fishing-boat pass in the channels on either side, and across the tideway to the east, the shingle beach runs in a long spit down to the mouth, dividing the river from the sea. It is a strange setting in the estuary, with the sea so close, the shingle, the mudflats, the marshes and the river surrounding it, and only a short run in the boat to isolate you from people. It is these features and, perhaps above all, the close relationship with Nature the island offers that convey a sense of magic when you step ashore.

On Havergate Island

The island is, of course, well known as a sanctuary for a range of different species of wader and sea bird, many breeding there, others on spring and autumn passage, and others, particularly ducks, wintering there. But undoubtedly Havergate, like Minsmere, the RSPB coastal reserve a few miles north, is known most of all for that elegant black-and-white bird with the long up-turned bill, the avocet. This long-legged, strikingly beautiful creature has become the symbol of the RSPB, not surprisingly since the society has done so much to recolonize the species since the bird's return to Britain after a lapse of a hundred years. It arrived at a Norfolk site in 1941 and appeared in Suffolk in 1947, beginning with four pairs each at Minsmere and Havergate, and since then most of the British population have bred at these two reserves. From the time the society purchased the island in 1948, the avocet colony there has steadily grown, and now it numbers a hundred pairs.

Avocets

The island covers over 260 acres and, it is thought, was formed during the sixteenth and seventeenth centuries, when the shingle spit cutting off the then busy port of Orford from the sea gradually extended south, developing into what is now the east bank of the estuary running three miles or so down to the entrance. It has mainly a farming history, maintaining first sheep, then cattle, which were ferried across from the mainland to graze it until 1939. Like so much of the Suffolk coastal estuary area, it was also associated with smuggling, and particularly with one of the most unpleasant of the smugglers, John Luff; the broken foundations of the cottage in which he is said to have lived still remain near the centre of the island. Just east across the channel on Orford Beach is the setting of the final act that brought the curtain down on the romance of Will Laud and Margaret Catchpole, when she was recaptured and Laud and John Luff were shot dead; a sorry tale to which I referred in Chapter 3.

During the war the island was used for military purposes, and during target practice damage was inflicted at the southern end which caused some flooding but with the fortunate result of making conditions suitable for avocets to breed. The reserve now consists mainly of six shallow lagoons with a water-level of around six inches controlled by sluices and containing small islands and mudflats for breeding birds and waders. All the lagoons are overlooked by hides, and there are clearly defined pathways to each below the grass-covered river walls and the lagoon embankments, so that one moves out of sight of the nesting- and feeding-areas and does not disturb the birds.

Although the reserve management has concentrated on the avocet, making the lagoons as beneficial as possible for breeding with strict regard to water-levels and salinity content, islands have been created and vegetation has been controlled to benefit the many other species of breeding and passage birds that use them. These include that familiar resident of the East Anglian estuaries, the oystercatcher, as well as ringed plovers and redshanks and various species of terns, while the passage-makers who find the habitat to their liking are black-tailed and bar-tailed godwits, greenshank, turnstone and curlew sandpiper.

Shelduck and mallard are in evidence throughout the seasons, and another inhabitant is the short-eared owl. Wintering ducks include widgeon, teal, pintail and shoveler. With such a variety of residents and migrants on the island there seems little accommodation for wintering geese; in fact, they are only occasional visitors; mostly they can be seen flying over the mainland marshes – brent, white-fronted and sometimes greylag. Swans are a familiar sight along most Suffolk estuaries, and the area around Havergate is no exception.

Saltmarsh borders the island outside the river walls, and below these green areas, mudflats, exposed at low tide, provide further rich feeding-grounds for waders. The only variation in this basic pattern is the shingle ridge which joins the southern area of Dove Point to the main part of the island. Here, in what is known as Doveys, is the sixth lagoon, the other five being located north of our landing-point. There is always an assistant warden and a voluntary helper or two on the reserve, and three small huts are sited near the beach landing to accommodate them.

The paths to the lagoon hides run through rough grassland, with here and there colourful patches of tamarisk and gorse and elder shrubs, ideal cover for hares, one or two of which were not unduly disturbed by our presence.

John Partridge and his resident deputy explained the problems and rewards of management as we moved north, one of the problems being the threat to nesting birds from such predatory mammals as the stoat and weasel, whose tracks were plainly visible at the edge of one shallow dike, although rats, which are more numerous, are the worst menace. On the other hand, the smaller mammals – such as water and field voles, common and water shrews – form the main source of food for the short-eared owls. Moles, we discovered, were more recent arrivals.

One path took us through one of the higher saltmarsh zones, a colourful carpet of sea purslane and sea lavender, just two of the 130 or so plant species the island supports. But it is the birds most visitors come to see, and certainly the hides provide a close-up view of the quiet activity going on in the lagoons. Binoculars are, of course, a must, but if you forget them, they can be hired from the reception centre, a short walk across the saltmarsh from the visitors' landing-stage. Each hide is well centred to give a pano-ramic view of the lagoon concerned. Certain islands and pools attract more birds than others, particularly in the area of the sluices. Apart from the avocets, feeding, resting or in flight, many of the other species I have mentioned are to be seen, and if you are there at the appropriate time, you may observe the fascinating ceremonies of some of their courtships.

A lagoon on Havergate Island

It was in the last hide overlooking the north lagoon that we found a swallow's nest, perched precariously on a beam, crammed with fledglings. A small window at the end of the hide was open for exit and entry of the adult birds, and our lagoon observations were accompanied by a close fly-past of the parent birds, interrupting our view from the windows. It was obvious from their constant to-ing and fro-ing that their intentions were to persuade us to leave – and quietly, regretfully, we did.

On the way back to Orford in the boat, John told us about the seals. There are usually two or three in the river, common seals I had observed on previous occasions when I was afloat. As with all the other wildlife species, there was no threat to their environment in this area from pollution.

John, who knows the river as he knows the streets of Orford, has lived in the town all his life and has been warden of Havergate since 1974, when he took over the exacting management task from his father, the late Reg Partridge, who had created the reserve for the RSPB following the return of the avocets and had remained warden for over twenty-five years. Apart from the layout of the habitats, the island's river defences had to be built up and maintained, and a setback with which he was confronted early in his wardenship was the disastrous flooding suffered by Havergate in the east-coast floods of 1953, when the embankments were breached. Reg Partridge and his band of voluntary helpers will be remembered for the competent way in which they handled the emergency, one of the worst natural disasters to hit the island and, indeed, other coastal areas, particularly Felixstowe, where forty people were drowned. It is difficult to imagine when observing Havergate now, midst its calm, remote setting, that such a catastrophic event occurred.

As we cruised back towards the north-east tip of the island, bar-tailed godwits were filleting the mudflats with their bills, a tern was flying overhead, an oystercatcher arguing with his mate in the saltings. The river around us, a rippling mirror of sunlight; the only disturbing sound the purr of the diesel engine, softened in the lullaby wash of water along the hull.

Looking back at the island as we followed the curve of the river, a pair of shelduck flighting across our wake, we had to conclude that in this tense, hustling age John had discovered the most enviable way of living. What did he think?

He smiled at us from the helm. 'I can't think of a better way of commuting to work,' he said. 'Can you?'

We are particularly fortunate in Suffolk to be blessed with so many lovely estuaries. Five in all, counting the Stour, dividing the county in the south and taking in the Orwell, the Deben and the Ore/Alde/Butley complex, to the Blyth near the northern boundary. Broad and narrow, they twist their way through mudflats and saltings, grazing marshes and gently rising wooded shores to receive, through barriers and sluices, the fresh-water rivers and streams that centre the low levels of delightful valleys inland.

Each estuary has its own special appeal and characteristics, but the Ore may be said to be unusual on three counts: it is the setting for Havergate Island; above Orford and without any break or barrier it becomes the Alde, and for ten miles or so from the entrance at Shingle Street to Slaughden Quay at Aldeburgh it runs parallel with the sea, so much of it at the southern end, within three or 400 yards of the beach. At Slaughden, where the Alde turns inland, the neck of shingle dividing river and sea is so narrow that they are almost within a stone's throw of each other, and the sea defences here are constantly under review. Another feature of this strange physical complex is that joining the Ore at the south-western end of Havergate is the Butley River, often referred to as Butley Creek, although to follow it on the tide as far as Gedgrave Cliff and beyond in a dinghy, 'river' seems a more appropriate designation.

The entrance to the Ore follows the pattern of its neighbours north and south, the Blyth and the Deben: narrow-mouthed, shifting banks, fast-running tides. Not only is the river more hazardous to enter but its setting presents a more dramatic scene: a seldom passive sea surfing on the great knolls of shingle exposed by the ebbing tide, the tumble of white water over the shallows, the bleak shingle spit of the seaward bank at North Weir Point with its deserted beaches, and on the mainland side shingle ridges melting into inlets of mud and saltmarsh reaching back to the river wall protecting the inland marshes; all contribute to its wild and hostile image. Even in the lower reach of the river the combination of tide and poor holding ground offers no friendly anchorage. The first safe haven for a boat to bring-up is on the south-west side of Havergate Island or tucked just inside the Butley River. It is characteristic of these estuaries that their boisterous entrances are in sharp contrast to their serene and verdant upper reaches.

The hamlet of Shingle Street, just south of the river mouth, with the sea at its front door and the marshlands at its rear, tends to emphasize the dramatic picture the sea and river portray. A

straggling line of cottages with a Martello tower at the southern
end, perched on the edge of the shingle beach, reminds me of a
small island habitation in its remoteness. But it is not as remote as
all that. In summer it is mildly popular with beach sunbathers,
although it remains free from holiday crowds, and there is so
much space anyway, that is easy enough to linger or walk alone.

Shingle Street

The village of Hollesley (pronounced Hosely), across the marsh
and on rising wooded ground, is no more than a mile or so away
and is easily reached from Woodbridge across Sutton Common,
passing the air base on the way. Another route from Woodbridge
through the villages of Sutton and Shottisham runs into Hollesley
from the southern end.

Hollesley is a village now seeing some modern residential
development, but it is perhaps best known for its large, open
institution for youthful offenders – the Hollesley Bay Colony,
located about a mile to the north-east, overlooking the Ore. You
get a hint of the huge area the establishment covers from the river,
but fortunately most of the large buildings are concealed by the
trees.

The river scene has changed little since the smugglers ferried
their illicit cargoes across the tideway from the beach. North of
the entrance on the mainland bank, where the shingle forms
shallow ridges into the saltmarsh, oystercatchers nest. A pattern
of little creeks and gullies indents the marsh to the river wall, and
in midsummer the green is coloured with sea lavender, sea

purslane and thrift. In places marsh samphire adds its red glow in the autumn, and on the east bank dividing river from sea, patches of sea kale, stonecrop and sea pea break up the dull monotony of the shingle.

A few hundred yards up river, where one of the tidal inlets meanders towards the grass-covered embankment, a small patch of mud and shingle forms a sheltered site where a common seal or two can often be seen resting or sunbathing. There are usually three or four of these delightful mammals in the estuary, and this seems to be their favourite haul-out spot. It is free from human interference and close to the deep water of the channel into which they can plunge should they sense any danger. A mile or so further up on the opposite bank, flying to and fro above the steep-to shingle, little terns are regularly observed fishing for eels.

But most of the interesting estuary birds and waders are found in the vicinity of Havergate. The river-wall path down from Orford to Chantry Point, where the cattle were once ferried across to the island, continues parallel with Havergate, eventually joining the Butley river. Although the lagoons are out of sight from the mainland embankment, there is always activity above them and in the saltmarsh and mudflats that skirt the island across this arm of the river which is called Long Gull.

Butley river is best appreciated from a dinghy, but there are walks down to it on either bank. The best views of its winding course and the valley itself are from the west side. Boyton, about three miles north-east of Hollesley, is a good place to start. The

Butley river

village is on a loop road and is well worth the slight detour, if not for the unexpected sight of a fine range of eighteenth-century almshouses on the way in, then for the view at the further end on the way out. Here, where the road turns sharply down to Capel St Andrew, is a farm track cresting the heights which opens up a vista of the Butley river, its marriage with the Ore, Gedgrave Marshes, Havergate Island and the sea.

Down the track, an easy walk takes you to Boyton Dock, about a half-mile up from the Butley river entrance. The substantial remains of the dock are another reminder of more leisurely days when the east-coast rivers were the trading waterways of the sailing-barge and farmer. There is ample water in this quiet spot for yachts to swing at anchor, and in summer there are usually one or two visiting craft off the dock. The path along the embankment takes you up river to Butley Ferry, where a few small boats lie, but there has not been a ferry here since 1920.

Whether you walk from the Ferry over Burrow Hill to the outlying fringe of Butley or drive from Boyton and Capel St Andrew, pause on the road skirting Butley Corner and note the Abbey Gatehouse. It is now privately owned, so cannot be seen in close-up, but it presents one of the finest examples of medieval skills in its beautifully carved stonework. This was the site of Butley Priory, founded in 1171, when a tributary of the river flowed close by and barges brought up the stone for its construction.

There is little trace of the ancient waterway now; the river runs about a mile to the east, and the next vantage-point that overlooks it, providing a lovely view down the valley almost to Gedgrave Cliff, is at Butley Mills. On the way from Butley Corner, note the thatch roof of the parish church. If it is unusual, it is not so surprising with such adequate supplies of reeds in the nearby river.

The next pause, if you are thirsty and it is opening time, is the Oyster Inn at the junction with the Orford road. The Oyster was for many years a traditional country pub with bench seats and barrels in the tap-room; it has now been renovated and refurbished in line with modern trends, although one or two original features remain. Nowadays it is difficult to find a real old country pub that has not had a facelift, but I suppose such places no longer provide a living for the landlord – or a profit for the brewer. But the Oyster now lives up to its name: you can usually find them on the menu.

Just down the road is Mill Lane and at the end of it Butley Mills. There have been watermills here since 1530. The present

red-brick building, no longer a working watermill but still used by
the miller, stands between the lane and the pool, the latter now
forming a quiet lake at the rear of the Mill House. The top of the
rise near the farm buildings presents a fine panoramic view
downstream of fields and marshes, islands of trees dressing
shallow hills and the winding course of the river bordered by the
encroaching reeds. Over the centuries, as trade and river traffic
declined, the upper reaches became heavily silted, but barges
continued to sail up to Butley Mills until 1914. Now, apart from a
thin tidal stream reaching the mill sluice, the head of the river is
lost under a blanket of reeds.

Down the lane from the mill is the hamlet of Chillesford on the
Orford road; on the outskirts, a few yards past the
creeper-covered mellow brick façade of the old Froize Inn, is
Friar's Walk. In fact, there are two walks here leading off the one
access from the road. Friar's Walk is a pleasant route to Orford
through Sudbourne Park, once a great sporting estate but long
since broken up; Froize Walk breaks away from the Orford path,
passing Decoy Wood to follow the river down on the east bank
for about a mile. While it presents another aspect of the river
valley, it does not link up with any other route, and the nearest
point at which you can get to the river again on the east side is
Gedgrave Cliff, which is reached via Orford along the Gedgrave
road.

Gedgrave Cliff and the little sandy beach, where barges once
unloaded their cargoes, are still completely unspoilt. This is
probably because there is no road down to them, and they are too
far away from the attractions of Orford and its quay, where most
visitors tend to spend their time. The Gedgrave road peters out
into a private track at the Hall, and then it is an undulating walk
across farmland to the river. Few visiting yachts go above Boyton
Dock, although there is sufficient water for a shallow draught
boat above the old ferry point. So the place remains delightfully
undisturbed, just as George Arnott found it forty years or so ago
when he summed it up in his book *Alde Estuary*: 'If you row up to
Gedgrave Cliff of an evening, you will not regret it. You will find
yourself in a world of your own, with the quiet, still countryside
around you. The evening sun warms the sandy beach and cattle
murmur from Burrow Hill opposite. Gedgrave is a remote spot
and likely to remain so. I hope it will never be "discovered".'

George Arnott's hope continues to be realized. The place
remains remote; few people seem to have discovered it. Perhaps
just as well for William Pinney, for in these unmolested
surroundings he lives in Ferry Cottage and farms the oysterage

Butley river at Gedgrave

just off the beach. The beds, which extend from the beach up river beyond the cliff, are marked by withies and buoys and a courteous notice board; any visiting yachtsman, therefore, should proceed with care.

The Butley–Orford Oysterage on Orford's Market Hill is a noted sea-food restaurant and shop (with a fine reputation for smoked fish and shellfish) which the Pinney family has run for many years. In his book *Smoked Salmon and Oysters*, the late Richard Pinney wrote an amusing account of how the business began and developed from his first oyster layings in Butley River soon after the war. William, together with his mother, continues the family tradition with a service and a menu that are known far beyond Orford.

The most striking feature in Orford is the castle, a great turreted tower which is in fact the keep, and all that remains of the original fortifications. It is a well-preserved public monument some ninety feet high, and from its battlements the strange configuration of the river with its long shingle bank separating it from the sea can be appreciated. The view encompasses the coast from Bawdsey to Aldeburgh, making the keep into a modern observation post of which the military took advantage during the last two wars.

The castle was built for Henry II over a period of eight years and was completed in 1173. The building-stone for the keep consists mainly of the local septaria, and the design was a new departure: at a time when most other examples were rectangular,

Orford Castle

Orford is polygonal, buttressed by three projecting towers, in one of which is the spiral staircase. The shape of the interior is circular, the living-quarters consisting of a lower and upper hall with side chambers including a chapel and kitchens and a basement with a well. The castle's history includes the legend of the Orford Merman, a strange creature half-man, half-fish, who was caught in the fishermen's nets and held prisoner in the castle at the time of the first custodian, Bartholomew de Glanville, a local landowner appointed by the king. The merman was held for several days and, although tortured, would not or could not speak. This did not prevent his eating ravenously each time he was offered food. He eventually escaped, returned to the sea and was never seen again. A modern version of him is depicted in the sign displayed at the Butley–Orford Oysterage.

Orford's other historic building, as dominant as the castle, is the church, standing on a rise just beyond Market Hill, its dimensions on a scale typical of the great wool churches of Suffolk. A church was built here about the same time as the castle, and the remains of the twelfth-century chancel still present some of the finest examples of Norman architecture at the east end of the present building most of which dates from the fourteenth-century. Its lofty interior and absence of pews give it a cathedral-like appearance, an ideal setting for the musical events associated with the Aldeburgh Festival. Benjamin Britten (the Suffolk composer) had many of his works performed here, including the first performance of *Noyes Fludde* and *Curlew River*. The church contains many notable items of interest, including some excellent sixteenth-century brasses.

I think of Orford as a charming waterside village, tending to forget that it was an important seaport in Tudor and Elizabethan times, when one of its major exports was wool. In the rash of development in recent years Orford has not been excluded, and much of its fringe residential expansion, limited though it is at present, is not at all in sympathy with the rural character of the lanes and alleyways around its centre and down Quay Street. However, Market Hill, where, in place of a market, there are parking-slots for cars, is still a very attractive square, flanked by red-brick and colour-washed cottages, a village shop or two, the Oysterage and two or three elegant houses. Two welcoming hostelries offer food and drink close by, the Crown & Castle Hotel and the King's Head.

Quay Street gives the impression of a broad avenue, with its long green, and at the end, near the river, the Jolly Sailor is very much a traditional pub that remains unspoilt, with a cosy kitchen bar reminiscent of a tap-room. It has had its share of natural disasters: it was flooded in the North Sea surge of 1953 up to the brass bar by the fireplace which records the event; ten years later a freak wind blew off most of the roof. On each occasion the local fire brigade came to the rescue, and the beer was soon flowing again. It has always been the 'local' for the watermen, fishermen and amateur sailors, and in summer most of the thirsty sightseeing visitors seem to make a bee-line for it.

A few steps away, over the hump which was made after the 1953 floods and which serves the same purpose as the river wall, is the quay. Incidentally, the smart chandlery with tea rooms above was converted from a dilapidated warehouse that once disfigured this end of the street. From the quay there are river-wall walks upstream, past the sailing club and down to Chantry Point and Long Gull channel opposite Havergate Island.

It was near Havergate Island on a bright winter's day that I had a pleasant encounter with a seal. I had the river wall to myself, the tideway was deserted. I had just climbed over a stile when a dark round head broke the surface not a stone's throw from the embankment. Common seals look most attractive and graceful in the water, a striking comparison with the ungainly movements of their bodies when they haul out. This one was staring at me as the tide took him upstream, so I called to him to come back. He kept me in focus and I kept calling as he drifted up on the tide some fifty yards or so, then he suddenly vanished below the surface. I was about to walk on when he reappeared opposite me. I began calling again and he continued to watch me as the tide took him up. He vanished again. I waited a few moments and he was back in the original position. How many times he repeated this exercise, staring at me from above the surface as the tide carried him away, then swimming underwater against it to reappear, and who first tired of it, I can't remember, but it was an interesting demonstration of the overwhelming curiosity of this fascinating sea mammal.

The quay is another of Orford's popular attractions. There is usually something of interest going on, while the static display of yachts and fishing craft on the mooring trots up and down river adds form and colour to the scene. A vehicular ferry operates between the quay and Orfordness, usually referred to by those familiar with the place as 'The Island'. The ferry is not a public conveyance, neither is Orfordness an island, but part of the ten-mile shingle spit extending from Slaughden down to the river mouth, although a long, straight creek cuts into it from the south. It is a pancake-flat foreland with a wide shingle beach topped by the lighthouse and divided by the creek, Stoney Ditch, from rough farmland at its broadest point opposite Orford. A small part of it at the southern end is farmed, some corn is grown and cattle are grazed in summer. The place has had a chequered military history for most of this century, and although the buildings are now dilapidated and deserted, it is still under the control of the Ministry of Defence and so out of bounds to the public.

Orford Quay

Orfordness has been used for a number of military experiments since the First World War. At that time an airfield was established mainly for the testing of aircraft armaments, although it was from a squadron based here that a German Zeppelin was shot down in June 1917. It continued as a defence establishment until the late 1970s. It was here that the early radar experiments were developed before this work was moved to Bawdsey in 1953. After the last war the Atomic Weapons Research Establishment moved in, and a variety of strange concrete installations appeared. After the AWRE departed in 1971, the Americans set up an experimental early warning system named Cobra Mist. The large building and the festoon of masts and wires were sited at the northern end of the spit on Lantern Marshes; but the results seemed to interfere with the radio equipment of ships rather than produce any effective early warning of approaching missiles, and after only three years the whole set-up was withdrawn, practically overnight. The Cobra Mist site was taken over by the BBC, and the World Service now goes out from there. The two landing-craft ferries, though not so busy as before, continue to service the crossing.

On the shore, beyond the graveyard of ruined buildings that dot the site, the gleaming red-and-white-banded column of the lighthouse stands out, a bright, isolated finger of colour across the bleak plateau. There has been a lighthouse of a kind here since the early seventeenth-century, after a night of disaster in 1627 when thirty-two ships were lost. The present tower, ninety-nine feet high, dates from 1792 and came under the control of Trinity House in 1836. White flashing every five seconds, it has a range of 15.5 miles. It was made fully automatic in 1959 and is monitored from the Trinity House depot at Harwich via landlines. Even so, a keeper is still required to make a regular weekly visit to run the emergency generator and check the other essential equipment should the main power supply fail, as well as being on call for any emergency, and Charles Underwood has been doing this part-time since the light was automated. He has worked in various capacities on this secret site for many years; now he is retired but continues his weekly routine visit to the lighthouse, and when we went over with him on a fine summer's day we could appreciate how hazardous his journey might be in winter.

When we took the ferry and climbed into the Land Rover near the landing-point, the lighthouse looked no more than a half-mile away, but the zigzag route the journey entailed turned out to be nearer two miles. The road soon turned into broken concrete lanes which deteriorated further when we had crossed the narrow bridge over the creek to end in a beach track at the lighthouse door. We had the impression of a wasteland of derelict buildings, paneless windows, crumbling walls – laboratories, testing-beds, accommodation block, buildings that for so long had played a secret role in the defence of the country.

Charles Underwood, who lives in Orford and has spent so much of his working life in this hive of military science, gave us a running commentary on past events that eventually led to the desolate village it is today, causing us to wonder when the ministry was going to hand it over to the stewardship that had designated the county coastline 'The Suffolk Heritage Coast'.

The bright paintwork of the lighthouse tower and the former keeper's lodge was in sharp contrast to what we had seen on the way, and this was emphasized by the spotless interior and shining brasswork. From the lantern room we traced the coastline from the Naze at Walton in the south to beyond Aldeburgh in the north, as well as the shipping route closing Harwich. Behind us the river, creeks and marshes dissolved into a gently rising wooded hinterland along the western horizon. The whole length of the spit was deserted; the pebble beach descending in ridges to the shingle tideline sparkled clean under the wash of the sea.

On the empty beach a little later, while the generator ran its test, we wondered when Charles, quite apart from his routine visits, was last called on to make what seemed to us a rather long and arduous journey in response to an emergency.

'Not since the main power supply failed in the great storm of '87.' He glanced approvingly along the lonely beach, changing the mood with a smile. 'But we sometimes come over for a quiet picnic on the beach,' he said.

From Orford the direct road north to Snape takes you through the village of Sudbourne; but whenever I am that way I use the Ferry Road from the village following the river up to Iken. This gently undulating route offers delightful views of the Alde's course

Iken

and its gradual change upstream after rounding Ferry Point, where a ferry once plied to Slaughden, into a broad estuary between wooded shores, lake-like when the tide is high, a twisting ribbon of water between extensive mudflats on the last of the ebb. Over forty beacons mark the tortuous channel on its way up to the sandy beach at Iken, sheltered by a little promontory graced by the church.

In his book *Suffolk Scene*, published before the Second World War, in which he was killed, Julian Tennyson wrote glowingly of the Alde around which and on which so much of his early life was spent:

> The loveliest part of the whole river is at Iken, where the church and rectory stand lonely on a little wooded hill at the head of the bay that curves sharply back beneath bracken and oak trees and steep, sandy cliffs ... Behind it are fields, woods and heaths stretching down to Orford, to the right of it the marshes and the distant sea. A huge expanse of river lies before you when you lean over the graveyard wall; the long, dark pine wood of Blackheath and the bay in the corner where widgeon gather in thousands on winter nights, seem at least two miles off; but wait till low tide and you will see the whole river fall away until it becomes a flat, shining ocean of mud with the channel a thin thread through the middle of it.

The overall picture that Julian Tennyson portrayed in his evocative book has changed over the years, but fortuntaely not too much around Iken. You can lean over the churchyard wall and still admire the same scene; the little bay and the verdant cliff touched by the curve of the river remain unspoilt. Some of the heathland has vanished under the plough, and the meadow sloping down to the shore is now a picnic area, but since it is all part of the Heritage Coast, its beauty should be secure.

From Iken the river winds a further two miles through prolific reed-beds to Snape Quay; but as most of the channel dries to a trickle at low water, you need to go up and return on the same tide unless you are staying alongside the quay for the night. It is a tricky sail either way, but the intriguing feature of this stretch of the tideway is well worth the effort. Barges still sail up to the quay, as they have since the early nineteenth-century, though they no longer carry cargoes, and in summer you can usually find one or two alongside. There is a picturesque riverside walk of about a mile from Iken to Snape Maltings, but it should be remembered that this is liable to flooding in places on some high tides.

Snape Maltings, now internationally known through the Aldeburgh Festival, is a huge complex of nineteenth-century industrial buildings that have developed over the last few years into Suffolk's star tourist attraction. From the red-brick, creeper-covered front to the fine concert hall, created by Benjamin Britten and Peter Pears, overlooking the marshes at the rear, the facilities available serve most interests. Music (with the Britten–Pears School for Advanced Musical Studies), art and crafts form the central feature, but there are shops to suit a number of tastes, a tea room, a wine bar and holiday courses on countryside subjects, as well as the programme of events in the concert hall itself. The maltings now offer some holiday accommodation and facilities for exhibitions and conferences, and there are plans in the air for a visitors' centre and even a hotel. All these facilities have been created in sympathy with the mellow character of the buildings, which are listed as being of architectural and historical significance, and as the site is also in a conservation area, any future developments will continue to be governed by the restrictions these designations impose.

The maltings were founded around 1850 by Newson Garrett, a member of a local industrial family, and his successful venture built Snape into a thriving little port that even attracted the railway via a branch line from Saxmundham. The archway at the front of the buildings recalls this period. The maltings continued working until 1965, after which some of the buildings were used for grain storage, mostly moved by road, although this is now being phased out. The past industrial link with farming and the sea is recalled in the inn sign of the Plough & Sail, the pub standing prominently at the approach to the quay where you might be tempted to take a refresher after touring the complex.

It is well known that the Aldeburgh Festival was founded in 1947 by Benjamin Britten and Peter Pears, together with Eric Crozier, and they were later joined by Imogen Holst. The early events took place in Aldeburgh in the Jubilee Hall, another reminder of Newson Garrett, who built it, in the local church and in those at Orford, Framlingham and Blythburgh. As the festival became established, a more permanent home was sought and Snape Maltings, conveniently near Aldeburgh, was an obvious venue. The largest of the malt-houses was leased and a fine concert hall created which was opened in 1967. Misfortune followed two years later, when the hall was gutted by fire, although the brick walls survived. It was rebuilt in time for the start of the 1970 Festival, and on both occasions was opened by Queen Elizabeth II.

The village of Snape is about a half-mile over the river bridge which practically adjoins the quay. The tidal limits are just above the bridge which replaced a lovely humped-back one dating from around 1800, destroyed to a chorus of protests from artists and conservationists when the new one was built nearly thirty years

Sea wall and river embankment, Slaughden

ago. The Crown Inn in the village was once a smugglers' haunt, and near the church, another half-mile to the north just across the Saxmundham–Aldeburgh road, a burial ship was discovered in the last century, smaller than the Sutton Hoo vessel but the grave dating from about the same time. In recent years excavation work has begun in this area, and a number of ancient artefacts have been discovered. It continues to be a site of importance to archaeologists, although it is not expected to reveal anything that rivals Sutton Hoo.

Aldeburgh is only five miles away, but before heading there I would be tempted to see more of the river along the north bank from Snape. From the bridge the river wall carries a snaking path about a mile to Snape Warren, where it moves up from the tideway through bracken and trees to join the 'sailor's path' to Aldeburgh. 'Sailors' paths' are long-established walks that derive their name from the cross-country route sailors took to town or village when their vessel was in port. The walk from Snape to Iken, already mentioned, is another path so named. This and the walk to Aldeburgh on the north side of the river are two of the loveliest in the area. From Snape Warren the path runs for about four miles through the pines of Black Heath Wood, skirting Hazelwood Marshes before reaching the main road near the golf club on the edge of the town.

Aldeburgh is smart, fashionable, prosperous but with a reserved, elegant air about it, retained from its Victorian past. It owed its beginnings as a holiday resort to the arrival of the railway in 1850, and by the time the branch line closed in 1967 its popularity had long been established. It is very much a residential town, but its rapid growth as a holiday venue in post-war years no doubt springs from the fame of its annual festival. It has, of course, a further attraction in that, like Southwold further north along the coast, it has the sea, river and marshes at its limits, which give it a dimension rarely matched elsewhere.

The town has some fine Victorian houses to the west of the High Street, some of them of mansion-like proportions, most in spacious, leafy grounds; a few more modern properties generously laid out are nicely situated with an outlook towards the river. This is a pleasantly quiet area, and 'Private Road' notices tend to keep it that way. High Street shops cater for every need, and there are wine bars, art galleries, a cinema and a festival booking-office; three very good hotels overlook the sea. All this and fresh fish to buy from the fishermen's huts fronting the road within a pebble's throw of the inshore fishing-boats hauled up on the beach. The lifeboat too is launched from the beach. It stands ready to swoop

Sailing on the Alde

down into the breakers at the command of a distress call. It was in the days of sail and oar that the lifeboat capsized, drowning the crew, and a plaque in the church records this tragedy.

The church also recalls more recent events associated with the town's famous resident, Benjamin Britten. A window representing three of his works, *The Curlew River, The Burning Fiery Furnace* and *The Prodigal Son*, is an expressive portrayal by John Piper, who designed many of the composer's stage sets. Benjamin Britten lies in the churchyard, close to his friends Peter Pears and Imogen Holst.

Aldeburgh was once a thriving port, though there is little left to signify this. Medieval Aldeburgh has long since been taken by the sea. Centuries of erosion all along this coast drowned so many ancient towns and villages, and the problem continues to require urgent defensive action. At Aldeburgh the Moot Hall, dating from the early sixteenth century, was originally in the centre of the town but is now within a few yards of the beach.

The sea-defence problem is vividly apparent at Slaughden. Little more than groynes and the concrete wall separate sea and river. Here was once a village with a shipbuilding and fishing industry, quays and warehouses. Shipbuilding was already in decline when George Crabbe, the poet, was born here in 1754. The son of a salt master, he worked unhappily for a time at Slaughden, and his early experiences no doubt bred the sombre mood evident in much of the work he later produced. He soon left home to seek his

Old barge jetty which once served the Aldeburgh Brickworks

fortune in London, but it was back in Aldeburgh more than twenty-five years later that he found fame. His work and his name were recalled to prominence some two centuries later, when Benjamin Britten based his opera *Peter Grimes* on Crabbe's poem 'The Borough'.

Little remains of the Slaughden Crabbe knew. The warehouses, the inn and the cottages have been washed away. The only relic to conjure up the past is the Martello tower, the northernmost of the Napoleonic defences, at the end of the sea wall. Slaughden still has a quay and a boatyard, mostly serving the sailing fraternity, although beach boats for the Aldeburgh fishermen have been built at the yard in recent times. The Aldeburgh Yacht Club and the Slaughden Sailing Club are based here, with a number of class racing boats, including a fleet of that lovely, long-established little craft the Dragon.

At Slaughden the north bank of the river is a tempting invitation to the walker and the naturalist. The river-wall path upstream lays open Aldeburgh Marshes and eventually a view of the broadening estuary as far as Iken church. A few steps further and a solitary focus-point recalling trading days under sail catches the eye: the decaying piles of the old barge jetty poke their timber stumps forlornly above the placid surface at high tide. The jetty once served the Aldeburgh Brickworks nearby, still a working industry.

It was across a stretch of the river not far from Slaughden that I saw a snowgoose, one which at some time, somehow, had strayed off course and had settled in residence with a colony of Canada geese – there are many such colonies along the Suffolk estuaries. I had seen the white goose before, inland, from my study window, prominent amongst the black-necked, brown-feathered Canada as they flighted in to settle on the stubble to feed for a brief interlude in the evening light. They appear each autumn, their familiar loud trumpeting call driving me out of the house to watch the flights glide down to the stubble fields across the valley. I had often wondered about the white goose amongst the great colony of eighty or more birds, never quite sure of its identity or from whence it came until by chance I noticed it in the colony on the Alde. Even now I can't be certain of identity or location. But does it matter? When they rise from the fields, dark shadows against the dying colours of a sunset sky, and fly north-east back into the dusky silence of the estuaries, all I can be sure of is that they form part of that mystery and magic that cannot be transcribed.

6

Reeds and Saltings

Heading up the River Blyth from Southwold harbour reminds me of the upper reaches of the Alde. Each river broadens out to resemble a quiet summer lake at high tide, and acres of mudflats, saltings and reeds at low water. If there is less of the Blyth estuary than of the Ore and Alde, its valley is a wide, open green of marshes and dikes, with here and there a wandering creek to freshen the wildlife habitats with every tide.

From Walberswick village on the south side of the narrow river entrance the marshes stretch down inside the coastline, studded with islands of birch and pine, to nudge the flanks of Dunwich Forest. Across the harbour to the north this moist landscape lays an open vista to the rising ground of Southwold Common and the spacious greens that edge the town. It is lovely country, and whether the choice is south or north or up river to Blythburgh and beyond, few walkers or naturalists, or even those content with glimpses from the roads, could fail to enjoy the varied scenes that make up this large conservation area.

Walberswick itself is a very attractive village, with a pleasant green, some beautiful old houses, terraces of red-brick cottages, two inns and a number of modern residences built on the outskirts. The church, too, catches the eye, since it appears to be built within the ruins of its predecessor. In fact, the present building dates from 1698 and incorporates the south aisle of the original fifteenth-century church whose ruins still dominate the east and north sides.

Walberswick is a popular location for artists and a paradise for youngsters, provided they are not seeking the amusements of the holiday fun-fair. This is a natural playground with its area of dunes, long sandy beach and muddy creek and the attraction of fishing-boats and pleasure craft coming and going over the fast-running tides in the harbour. August each year is the highlight for the children, when the village sponsors the National Crabbing Championship; young competitors gather at the timbered footbridge over the creek to vie with each other for the largest crab caught without using hooks or nets, and afterwards returned unharmed to the water. This jolly event always raises a substantial sum for the village play area.

Fishermen's huts at Walberswick

The creek marks the old course of the river which ran south to the port of Dunwich, which, along with the rest of the old town, has long since been swallowed by the sea. Medieval Walberswick was a sheltered haven on the bend of the river; it was an important trading-post for farm produce, and a major centre for the fishing industry. Like Southwold and Blythburgh, Walberswick's outlet to the sea was through Dunwich, which enacted increasing levies on its shipping as the port authorities endeavoured to combat the creeping coastal erosion and the silting of the harbour. The port continued to decline, and the reluctant association Blythburgh, Southwold and Walberswick had with Dunwich was finally broken in 1590, when Walberswick and Southwold combined to cut the present entrance. The narrow waterway above the sluice of the creek which runs through the marshes towards Dunwich Forest is still called 'the Dunwich river'.

Derelict wind pump on Walberswick marshes

Whenever I cross the creek and stand on the dunes or the high beach at Walberswick and look south along the lonely curve of the shoreline to Dunwich cliffs, with distant glimpses of village roofs amongst the trees, my eye is always offended by the ugly blob of the nuclear power station at Sizewell. It appears as a concrete block at the end of this long coastal sweep, just south of Dunwich, and until recently was the only blemish on this lovely shoreline. Now, at the time of writing, after years of controversy this old Magnox station, known as Sizewell A, has a PWR neighbour (Sizewell B) rising under the tall cranes clearly visible in the view south. The long-running arguments for and against this second massive structure exploded again when plans for a third station (Sizewell C) splashed over the county and national media. It was only when the real cost of nuclear power was realized, in the run-up to the privatization of the electricity industry, that the plans for C were abandoned.

It seems it is not the risk, the further intrusion into a rural community and the molesting of the countryside, the traffic and the human and material influx, but economics. The fact that just north, on the doorstep of this huge power complex, is the beautiful RSPB reserve of Minsmere makes no difference either. Despite the relief of conservationists and other bodies at the abandonment decision – which, according to reports at the time of writing, may yet turn out to be no more than a postponement – Sizewell B continues to rise and has again drawn their undivided attention.

So much for the Heritage Coast – where even a fisherman's hut appears out of place! Better to turn the other way …

Southwold harbour is nearer Walberswick than it is to the town, and most of the marine activity is along Blackshore on the Southwold side. Boat stages line each bank of the river as far as the Bailey footbridge almost a mile upstream, yachts on the south side and mainly fishing-boats along the opposite bank. The harbour has a small force of professional fishermen, and the huts lining Blackshore within yards of the stagings provide sales counters for the daily supply of fish.

Southwold Harbour

The river is narrow, but the fast-running tides are not conducive to 'messing about' in a boat; but the ferryman will take you across. A ferry has linked Walberswick with Southwold for centuries, first by rowing-boat, then from around 1885 by a chain and hand-cranked platform later replaced by steam power. This ferry closed in 1941, but the craft used in the seasonal service still operating is again provided by a rowing-boat.

If the ferry is not available, there is the Bailey bridge which links the path from Walberswick Common to Blackshore. This bridge is sited where the old swing bridge, destroyed for obvious reasons during the war, once carried the Halesworth–Southwold Railway which ran along the edge of the Blyth valley through Wenhaston and Blythburgh to Walberswick Common, then over the river to Southwold. It was noted for its tramcar carriages, made for use in China but which somehow ended up on the Halesworth–Southwold line, pulled by three light tank engines.

The Walberswick to Southwold ferry stage

Cross the bridge and just downstream of it, straddling the river wall separating Blackshore from the marshes, is the Harbour Inn, a pleasant waterside pub that can boast its defiance of the 1953 floods by recording high up on its wall the level to which the waters rose. Nearby the inn is the Southwold Sailing Club, and further along this bank, apart from the many fishermen's huts, is the RNLI inshore lifeboat station and a boatyard.

Upstream of the footbridge, paths, bridleways and narrow lanes provide splendid views of the river, taking you close to the saltmarsh and reedbeds, while the embankments either side of the main channel can be followed to the point where the river broadens into a shallow estuary that at high tide fills the valley.

I have said before that the best way to appreciate a river and its surroundings is to sail on it. This is not so easy in most upper reaches, where the depth of water and other natural restrictions limit you to a dinghy. Certainly you could not take a sailing-boat under the low Bailey bridge at Southwold harbour without lowering the mast. A small open boat is the answer, and John

Buckley, who runs the boatyard on Blackshore, provided it: a pretty little double-ender, sixteen feet in length, not exactly reminiscent of an old ship's lifeboat, although this was the role for which it was built in 1901. Whatever its long history, it must have been caringly maintained, for there was little hint of its great age. The light diesel engine made little fuss and little disturbance in the wide, open environment of the river valley; not enough, anyway, to push the cormorants off their perches on isolated stakes upstream or to move the statue-like herons in the shallows.

Just above the bridge, Buss Creek opens off on the north side to meander through the marshes, its narrow course taking it round the back of Southwold, dividing the town (and almost making it an island) from the village of Reydon, although when you drive over the road bridge from one to the other you hardly notice the creek. Up river a mile or so beyond the derelict wind pump are the remains of Reydon Quay. From here an old wagon track runs across the grazing marshes to join Quay Lane, where the Quay Inn once entertained visiting sailors – smugglers, too, since its isolated location made it a convenient trading-post for contraband. A gnarled gatepost recalls its presence, for the inn was long ago converted into a private residence. Alterations and

John Buckley and companion

The Old Quay Inn, Reydon Quay, now a private residence

extension have changed its appearance but a small part of the original building has been retained, incorporated at one end of the house.

Another half-mile and we were threading the narrow channel which hugs the south shore, with a vast expanse of shallow water covering the mudflats and saltmarsh to the north as far as the inlet of Wolsey Creek almost a mile away. With so much water and so little depth and the absence of marks to denote the channel except for here and there the half-submerged remains of what had once been the river embankments, it seemed an unlikely playground for the waterskier; but John Buckley told us that on more than one occasion he had pulled a ski boat off the mud and towed it back to the harbour. In any event, such a sport seemed out of place in this peaceful setting, where the pace has for long been set by Nature and where the quickest movement is the flight of a bird.

The inter-tidal mudflats of these broad upper reaches, with acres of saltmarsh coloured in season with sea lavender, sea purslane and sea aster, are important feeding-grounds for wildfowl and wading birds. Widgeon and teal winter here, joining the more familiar mallard and shelduck, and such regular waders as redshank, oystercatcher and dunlin. We were too early for the winter arrivals, but the resident duck and waders were constantly around us as we twisted and turned across Angel Marshes, following the channel to Blythburgh Bridge.

Wherever you are around Blythburgh (down the river or on the A12 road either side of the village), the parish church is a magnificent focal-point. It is a huge, cathedral-like building, dating from the fifteenth century, when the wool trade flourished in Suffolk and when Blythburgh was a teeming maritime town, its quays lined with ships, its steets with market stalls, a boisterous place with its own gaol and a courthouse which is now the White Hart Hotel, a fine inn with gardens running down to the river. As in many other ports of the period, Blythburgh's decline rapidly set in when larger ships were built, their draught too deep for the shallow river channels, and owners and builders sought deep-water ports elsewhere. The silting of the river and the decline of Dunwich hastened the town's decay, and after the marine trade had gone, so did most of the inhabitants.

Angel Marshes, Blythburgh

It is a quiet village now, apart from the intrusion of the A12, but the dominance of Holy Trinity church is a striking reminder of Blythburgh's busy and populous past.

Inside the church, the cathedral-like impression is even more marked; light, spacious, uncluttered, with bare areas of stone-flagged floor, its huge proportions present an air of simplicity and calm. There is little to suggest two noted turbulent periods in its history in its appearance now – until you look closer. The carved wooden angels high up in the roof were one of the targets of the church-wrecker Dowsing's henchmen (the damage was repaired in

recent years by American generosity); brasses were removed and
statues destroyed. It is said the wreckers even tethered their horses
to the pillars of the nave. Remains of tethering-rings and the
disturbed brickwork of the flooring below can still be seen.

Over a hundred years before Dowsing's arrival, in 1577, a great
storm struck the church during a Sunday service. According to
records, this storm '... cleft the door, and returning to the steeple,
rent the timber, brake the chimes, and fled towards Bongay, six
miles off'. The steeple crashed down, killing a man and a boy and
injuring members of the congregation. All bore marks of scorching.
Legend has it that this was the work of the Devil in person and that
the scorchmarks still to be seen on the north door were made by his
fingers as he left the church. Holy Trinity and the church of St
Edmund at Southwold are two of the very few churches to possess a
'Jack-o'-the-clock', a painted wooden figure in medieval armour
whose original function was to strike the hours with his axe.

The church stands on a rise just west of the road bridge and close
to the river, which from this point on forms a narrow tideway
edged by reeds almost ten feet tall. After a few turns the reeds
diminish and the river takes a long, curving course up the valley to
the tidal limits at Blyford Bridge, five miles or so to the west. There
is a fine walk along the river bank which in places tracks close to the
route of the old Southwold Railway. About two-thirds of the way

Blythburgh church

River Blyth at Blyford

upstream the path crosses to join the north bank at Bulcamp Bridge. Here there is a choice of continuing alongside the river to the road at Blyford Bridge or joining the path crossing the grazing marshes from the Bulcamp road (B1123) near Blythburgh hospital on the north side of the valley to Wenhaston on the south side, since all link up at the bridge.

Wenhaston is a pleasant, straggling village in a pretty setting, with some modern residential developments mostly located to enjoy the delightful views over the valley. The church is noted for its Doom, a large, impressive timber panel painted around 1400 which is said to have been the work of a Blythburgh monk. The village joins Blyford at the river bridge; a few hundred yards further along the lane the Queen's Head inn overlooking the green is conveniently placed to quench the rambler's thirst.

From here the road back along the north side of the valley (B1123) joins the A12, with Blythburgh to the right to complete the circle, or left up the hill to leave the main road again for Southwold.

This is a pretty run to the town, with glimpses of the estuary, and paths and a byway down to the shore. The road skirts a nature reserve (Reydon Wood is another) and turns to cross Wolsey Bridge, where the creek embankments nudge the road. Approaching Reydon outskirts, Quay Lane opens off to the right and peters out into the wagon track leading to Reydon Quay.

Southwold would charm the most demanding visitor, providing the demand was not for entertainment of the boisterous kind. It is as much residential as it is a holiday venue, with all the requirements expected of a small seaside town. There are a number of hotels, one of the largest adjoining the market-place in the town centre. There is a lively Summer Theatre, art galleries and a small museum. Numerous greens give the town a spacious, uncluttered air, complemented by the neat cliff-top North Parade, promenade and long, sandy beach. Clean, narrow streets are lined with cottages and houses, many of them Georgian, some displaying neat windowboxes in season, adding to the attraction of the red-brick and colourwash walls and red-and-blue pantile roofs. Just off the market-place, rising above the roofs which cluster around it and dominating the town, is the white tower of the lighthouse. Like that at Orfordness, the light is automated, and it has a range of eighteen miles. It could not be more conveniently placed for the routine check by the keeper, and whenever I pass it, I recall the journey entailed by his Orford colleague.

Southwold

The other dominant building is the fifteenth-century church of St Edmund nearby, with a tower but a few inches lower than the lighthouse. Finely proportioned in the Perpendicular style, its exterior noted for some fine flintwork, the whole of the building inside is flushed with light and colour – with the exception of the west window, all the Victorian stained glass windows were blown out during the last war and replaced with clear glass. A striking feature is the early sixteenth-century painted screen which spans the width of the church and which must be one of the finest examples of its kind from the period. The 'Jack-o'-the-clock' here operates in a similar way to the one at Blythburgh; at the tug of a rope he strikes the bell to announce the service. He is also employed to proclaim the arrival of the bride at her wedding.

The Southwold Jack has another claim to fame, having been adopted as the trademark of the local brewery. Adnams have been brewing some of the best beer in the country since 1872, when the family took over a small existing brewery. A traditional feature they brought back some twenty years ago was the horse-drawn dray. Used for local deliveries, the drays are a delightful contribution to the attractions of the town.

On Gun Hill, which slopes up to the cliff to form one of the loveliest greens overlooking Sole Bay, six eighteen-pounder guns remind you of Southwold's battle-scarred past. They have been stationed there since 1745, but the emblems on them of the Tudor rose and crown confirm their earlier origin. They are said to have been presented to the town by the Duke of Cumberland when he landed at Southwold on his way from Scotland to London in 1745. During the 1914–18 war, when the Germans shelled the town, claiming that the guns were fortifications, they were removed and hidden for the duration; and again in the last war they were rushed into hiding and saved from becoming scrap metal when every available piece was taken to aid the war effort.

Southwold has seen many bloody sea battles over the centuries but nothing like the carnage created in the Battle of Sole Bay in 1672, the most outstanding event in the town's history. The Dutch fleet of 138 ships under the command of de Ruyter surprised the British and French forces anchored in the bay. Many of the Allied fleet of some 150 ships slipped their cables and sailed without their full complement, as many of the sailors were ashore, probably worse the wear for drink, having spent the previous day (Whitsun) in the taverns. The battle raged all day, the townsfolk lining the cliffs anxiously awaiting the outcome. Thousands were killed, hundreds of wounded from the three fleets were brought ashore. The Dutch fleet withdrew under cover of darkness, and despite the casualties of men and ships, the battle proved to be indecisive.

As you would expect, the battle is well represented in Southwold Museum, housed in a little building which in itself could be a museum-piece – a neat Dutch-gabled cottage across the green from the church. There are many items from Southwold's past, including a collection of Southwold Railway exhibits. The paintings and plans of the famous sea fight are a special feature, highlighting the battle formations, the whole presenting an absorbing picture of the events that occurred on that day.

The museum is run by the Southwold Archaeological and Natural History Society and is of necessity restricted to specific opening times; but the Sailors' Reading Room, overlooking the sea at the end of East Street, always appears to have an open door. The room is a miniature museum in itself, recording some of Southwold's maritime history, in which fishing has played such an important role over the centuries. You will usually find some retired fishermen at the reading table yarning over a card game or catching up on the news in the daily papers. The walls of the room are festooned with paintings, prints and old photographs of ships and sailors, as well as brightly painted ships' figureheads. On the side tables there are models of ships and beach boats, including an impressive scale model of *Bittern*, Southwold's most famous beach yawl.

The beach yawls, were a familiar sight along the Suffolk and Norfolk shores. They were owned by the beach companies, whose function was to service ships off the coast with supplies and pilotage and assist any vessel in difficulty. There was keen competition between the companies for this work, which became even more intense when a ship was in trouble, for their major objective was salvage, although in the process they also saved a great many lives. The yawls were impressive craft, fast, double-ended open boats between forty and seventy feet in length, their large lugsail rig requiring skilful handling. The *Bittern*, built in 1890 and forty-nine feet long, was reputed to be the fastest craft of her type on the coast. Although she has long since gone, her rudder remains, displayed outside the Sailors' Reading Room.

Down past the greens from Gun Hill and Ferry Road takes you back to the harbour. The Suffolk Wildlife Trust has a small centre here with, amongst other interesting items, photographic displays of the wildlife and fauna of the surrounding area. Walberswick and Southwold are fortunate in having their estuary and so much of the surrounding countryside safeguarded for all to enjoy.

The Blyth, the northern estuary of the county, is perhaps the least of the regions subject to pressures, although even in these more rural areas expanding recreational activities and holiday caravan sites are always jostling for accommodation. The problem of harmonizing the conflicting interests and at the same time safeguarding the natural environment for the appreciation of all is a continuing subject for study by the various conservation bodies and local authorities.

In their illustrated publication *The Suffolk Estuaries*, the Suffolk Wildlife Trust reports in detail on the effect most human activities have on the ecology of the estuaries and suggests guidelines for the future designed to mitigate their impact. In its conclusion the report states:

> Safeguarding the important species and the communities that inhabit the Suffolk estuaries requires the conservation and sensitive management of the whole ecosystem. In order to harmonise the conflicts that exist, it is clear that each user group must become more accountable for their activities. This requires co-operation and co-ordination between the various user groups and interested parties, and a deeper understanding of the wider impact of each operation. The formation of a user group for each estuary, and particularly the Orwell and Stour, which are subject to the greatest pressures, would help secure the future of their wildlife.

It would also help to ensure that indefinable quality that I have always interpreted as the magic of the estuaries.

7

The Broadland Waterways

If Norfolk lacks the estuaries that break up the coastline and hinterland of Suffolk and Essex, it makes up for the loss of these impressive features with the Broads. Broadland is a strange and fascinating area of around 200 square miles between Norwich and the coast, patterned with shallow waterways, mysterious fens, moist, tangled woodland and dike-riven grazing marshes that form an enchanted landscape under a wide open sky.

This low plateau of land and water fans out from the ports of Lowestoft and Great Yarmouth, adding an enticing dimension to the backdrop of these busy commercial and holiday resorts. From Hickling Broad and Horsey Mere in the north via Breydon water to Oulton Broad, within the Suffolk border, in the south, the waterways vein the coastal belt and network the country westward to Norwich, Coltishall and Wroxham, with their southern boundary running inland along the Waveney Valley to Beccles and beyond.

The origin of the Broads was for long wrapped in mystery. There was no certain explanation of how these shallow meres, most of them linked to the rivers, had been created. The general view was that they were a natural development, and this was accepted until the early 1950s, when research established that they were man-made. They consist of peat pits, dug in medieval times to meet the fuel demands of what was then a densely populated area. The rising sea-level flooded the workings during the fourteenth century, and this turn of Nature formed the watery landscape we see as the Broads today.

There are some fifty of these shallow lakes, ranging in size from the 300-acre expanse of Hickling Broad to small areas of reed-fringed water of no more than an acre or two. Some are completely isolated but most are fed and inter-connected by the main rivers, the Bure and its tributaries the Thurne and the Ant, and the Yare and the Waveney.

The Broads have a character and an atmosphere that are hard to describe. There is little to compare with them. Even the sheltered upper reaches of the estuaries south of the border do not possess the strange, mystical atmosphere created in so many places, where land and water merge so indefinably. Reed beds, alder swamps and wet, tangled woodland make it difficult to pinpoint the boundary between what is land and what is water. These confined areas, festooned with vegetation and intersected by narrow channels reaching into placid, tree-sheltered lakes, are a contrast to the miles of open landscape where the river banks protect a green plateau of marshland alive with sheep and cattle. In fact, the only small part of the Broads that reminds me of the estuaries to the south is Breydon Water.

Breydon is a four-mile stretch of salt tidal water just west of Yarmouth into which flow the three rivers: the Bure, winding through the northern heart of Broadland and joining Breydon at its eastern end; the Yare, which is the route to the sea from Norwich, and the Waveney from Beccles, both of which merge with the estuary at its western head. Here on the rising ground is Burgh Castle, the ruins of a Roman fortress built at the time when the sea covered the marshes and it stood at the mouth of a great estuary which extended to Norwich and Beccles.

Breydon, all that remains of this ancient estuary, is the odd-feature-out in Broadland; it is an area of extensive inter-tidal mudflats and saltings, a feeding-ground for wildfowl and waders. The deep-water channel is clearly defined by large coloured marker posts, so there is no excuse for the holiday sailor who strands his hire cruiser on the mud, although many still do, probably mocked by the cormorants who sit smugly on the posts drying their wings.

If the tidal influence is perhaps dramatic here, it is much less in evidence in the upper and middle reaches of the rivers, where the rise and fall ranges from around eighteen inches to three feet. The tidal streams vary in strength from less than a half knot to around four knots, depending on how close you are to Breydon Water, while on the Broads themselves the influence is minimal and to moor in the middle of one of these lovely lakes means no more than dropping a weight, thus avoiding the weed on the bottom which an anchor would bring up.

Berney Mill from Breydon Water

The last place on which we let go the weight was the placid surface of Bargate Water. This is part of Surlingham Broad (owned by the Norfolk Naturalists Trust) near Brundall, and the last Broad upstream off the Yare. Through the encroachment of vegetation over the years, Bargate is all that remains of navigable water at Surlingham; it is fed by two narrow channels from the river and peacefully surrounded by reed swamp and fen. Since we were there at the tail-end of the season, 'peaceful' is the right adjective.

It was a late autumn day under a cloudless sky, so quiet you could hear a cork pop on the only other boat, moored near the reeds; so hot in the cockpit that we had to quench our thirst below. From the skipper's private yacht berth we had moved out into the river past busy Brundall boatyards and riverside bungalows to lunch in the stillness of the Surlingham backwater, before proceeding up river to Bramerton, although once we had settled on Bargate Water no one seemed in a hurry to leave.

These higher reaches of the Yare, with their tumble of foliage caressing the banks eventually giving way to gently rising slopes on the approaches to Bramerton Woods End, reminded me of the upper reaches of the Thames. There was little to blur the picture of this delightful part of the Yare Valley. On the way a cruiser or two, here and there a sailboat; a lone angler on the bank, and upstream a heron at the water's edge, both with the same idea. A reed-thatched house standing back from the river, a reed-thatched boathouse at the head of the dike; but no sign of movement. No

transistors blaring, no boisterous crews in funny hats, almost
deserted waterways. The scene had that quiet, end-of-season look
when you have the space and time to appreciate that subtle quality
inherent in this watery landscape that makes the Broads such an
unusual experience.

Broadland is also remarkable for its rich variety of wildlife: its
wetland habitats are a haven, perhaps the only remaining one in
the country, for a number of rare species. It is the home of
Britain's largest butterfly, the swallowtail. That rare bird the
bittern, not often seen but frequently heard, with its identifying
penetrating boom reminiscent of a distant foghorn, nests in the
extensive reedbeds, which are also the homing-grounds of that
handsome flyer the marsh harrier. Several species of plants rare in
many parts of Britain are quite common in this habitat, including
milk parsley, the crested buckler fern and the fen orchid.

The area has for long been a naturalist's paradise – and of
increasing concern to the conservationist. Much of the marshland
has been reclaimed; in fact, reclamation has gone on for many
years. In the heyday of the windmill, windpumps, similar in
appearance to the old cornmills, were used to pump the water from
the marshes into the rivers to drain the land for cattle and sheep
grazing. Diesel and electric pumps are used today, but many of the
old marsh mills have been restored and, along with the derelict
towers, remain an interesting feature of the landscape. During and
since the war extensive tracts of marshland have been brought into
agricultural use for grazing and arable cultivation, with the

Surlingham Broad

consequent effect on the river environment; but one of the major pressures is apparent in the recreational use of the 125 miles of lock-free navigable waterways.

The Broads really began to develop as a sailing holiday venue in the 1920s and thirties, and when I first visited them just before the war, the hire fleets (and privately owned boats) consisted mainly of sailing-craft which had little or no effect on the river environment. In any event, they were comparatively small in numbers. Since the war the popularity of sailing has brought about a massive increase in boat-ownership and boating holidays all round the country, and on the Broads the traffic has increased to such an extent that the quiet waterways out of season have, during the long holiday months, become almost as busy as the roads.

During the season some 2,000 craft are available for hire, the majority of them motor cruisers, and each year over a quarter of a million holiday sailors step aboard a boat to explore this wonderland of waterways. Apart from the great seasonal influx, there are over 7,000 privately owned craft, although like many other personally owned boats elsewhere, most of these are sailed only occasionally. In addition, there are the water buses which ply the rivers with thousands of sightseers each year, while day-trippers hire the scores of self-drive launches available from such holiday bases as Wroxham, Potter Heigham and Oulton Broad among others.

The effects of recreation and pollution over many years have dramatically damaged the natural environment. Water quality has deteriorated, in some measure due to the use of nitrate fertilizers, and river walls are constantly in need of repair. Increasing numbers of anglers, ornithologists and ramblers tread the river banks. One of the most serious problems is created by the intense traffic in powerboats: the continuous wash of these craft is a major contribution to the erosion of the river banks, which in many places have had to be reinforced with unsightly piling, particularly where they protect low-lying agricultural land. The wash and propeller disturbance in such shallow waters also increases the rate of mud deposition on the Broads and rivers.

The River Yare at Bramerton

The difficulties of harmonizing the interests of public recreation with conservation have been relieved in a number of areas by the work of the various conservation organizations – the Norfolk Naturalists Trust, the Nature Conservancy Council, the Countryside Commission and other bodies, including local authorities, which have worked together with the Broads Authority to deal with the environmental problems that affect the whole region.

Brundall, River Yare

The Broads Authority was set up in 1978 with the objective of establishing Broadland as a national park, and although it has played a very active role over the years, it was not until April 1989 that it was officially launched in the heart of the region it was formed to protect. The ceremony, conducted by the chairman of the Countryside Commission, took place at Ranworth Broad, a Norfolk Naturalists Trust reserve and a splendid example of the results of conservation. With the ever-increasing pressures on the Broadland environment, the Authority has a continuing task of dealing with the urgent problems still to be solved.

The Norfolk Naturalists Trust is the oldest county-based voluntary organization in Britain to serve the cause of nature conservation. Founded in 1926, it now protects 6,500 acres in various parts of the county, including areas of the north Norfolk coast, as well as managing a number of Broadland reserves.

Ferry House Inn, River Yare

Ranworth Broad, on the middle reaches of the Bure, and Hickling Broad, off its tributary the Thurne and almost within scent of the sea, are two good examples of the trust's management. Ranworth, part of the Bure Marshes National Nature Reserve, which also includes Cockshoot and Malthouse Broads, is some 320 acres and is set in one of the most important wetland reserves in the country. Follow the nature trail through the mysterious wonderland of oak wood, swampland and reedbeds to the open, lake-like surface of water where a floating conservation centre awaits you. This unusual thatched timber building moored on pontoons adds another touch of magic to the

Hickling Broad

surroundings and houses an exhibition that takes in Broadland's natural history and explains the problems involved in safeguarding its future. From the upper floor there are excellent views over the reserve.

Hickling Broad, the largest stretch of open water in Broadland, fringed by wader pools, fen, woodland and grazing marsh, covers in all over 1,300 acres. In summer Hickling is the flighty playground of the swallowtail butterfly; other residents at this time include common and little terns, oystercatchers and, since their first arrival in 1982, avocets. Barn owls and tawny owls are amongst the permanent residents; migrants who are regular visitors are the spoonbill, osprey and black tern; and at all times there are many species of duck.

We found the well-marked walking-trails an exciting tramp even in a grey, late-autumn drizzle. Apart from one other wet observer we had the woodland, dikes and hides overlooking the scrapes (artificial lagoons) to ourselves and eventually settled down to dry out over a flask of coffee in the observation hut on the reed-fringed edge of Deep Dyke, which links Hickling Broad with Heigham Sound.

Hickling is managed jointly by the trust and the Nature Conservancy Council and is one of the most important as well as one of the most interesting ecological sites. Apart from the variety of fauna and flora, including the rare marsh orchid, over fifty acres of reed and sedge are harvested each year; the water trail, run for visitors during the summer season aboard what is thought to be the last reed-lighter (a traditional boat used for carrying cut reeds) offers an opportunity to learn something of this age-old method of marsh management. In fact, the continuing demand for reed and sedge (the latter being used for the capping of thatched roofs), which are harvested on a commercial basis in many areas, is welcomed by the conservationist, since it helps to maintain many of the wildlife habitats.

To appreciate to the full the Broads and the rivers that connect them, you need to be waterborne, and a boat will give you the whole picture. But having said that, it doesn't mean you miss out altogether when exploring by road. Most of the minor roads that cross the flat landscape will suddenly reveal a glimpse of water, and in many places across a field of corn or a grazing pasture the upper spread of a white or coloured sail gliding above the distant embankment will remind you where you are. But it is the network of lanes that will introduce the landsman to the essence of the Broadland scene – winding off from waterside villages to meander through grazing marshes and wet woodland to join a nature reserve or to fade away at a lonely river bank, a watery cut or a derelict windpump.

Most visitors get their first introduction to the Broads at Wroxham. Situated on the upper reaches of the Bure and some seven miles north-east of Norwich, Wroxham is the best-known and probably the busiest centre of the many throughout the region. It is the capital of Broadland, and its boatmen were the first to see the network of waterways as a potential magnet for the holiday sailor. From here the first very small fleet of hire yachts began to spread their sails before the First World War. Since the last war, sailing and the holiday charter industry have mushroomed at every boating location, and the Broads have certainly had their share. All summer

Wroxham is thronged with people whose needs are catered for by a variety of services – booking-agents, boatyards, chandlers, sailmakers and shops (including Roys, 'the biggest village store in the world'), while the yacht basins hum with the coming and going of all classes of craft.

Wroxham is just one of the easily accessible inland centres to give the motorist a lively welcome to the Broads. From the coast, Oulton Broad, adjoining Lowestoft, and the Bure and Breydon Water at Yarmouth provide entries from the A12.

Oulton Broad

My favourite route from Suffolk is across the Waveney Valley through Beccles. This is the southern boundary of Broadland, and Beccles is another of those riverside towns with an early maritime history. Its origins go back to beyond the eleventh century, when it was a booming fishing-port, rendering 30,000 herrings a year to the abbey of St Edmunds. Four great fires during the sixteenth and seventeenth centuries destroyed much of the town, and little remains today of its early architecture. Modern Beccles is a bustling place with some industry and much traffic; river traffic, too, which is perhaps more acceptable, throngs its waterway in summer, and a spacious quay welcomes holiday sailors to the town.

Prominently set on high ground rising from the river, a particularly attractive aspect of the waterfront above Beccles Bridge, are the red-brick Georgian houses with their long gardens sweeping down to private moorings occupied by smart launches or elegant cruisers. One of the more unusual features in the town, and an impressive landmark from the Norfolk side of the river, is the separate bell-tower of St Michael's, set beside the church. From the top of this massive ninety-foot structure there are magnificent views over the marshes. A romantic touch recorded here is that Edward Nelson and Catherine Suckling, who became the parents of Lord Nelson, were married in the church, and so was Aldeburgh's famous son George Crabbe.

A few miles west of Beccles is Bungay, a smaller town but of a similar character, its narrow streets flanked by a huddle of shops, pubs and houses, surrounding the remains of its twelfth-century castle. It is one of the most attractive towns in Suffolk; set on a height above the river, it encompasses sweeping views across the green plateau of marsh and meadowland bordering the county boundary.

Bungay was the town to which the great storm 'fled' after wrecking the church at Blythburgh in 1577. In Bungay it struck the church of St Mary's and in the midst of the havoc and confusion revealed the Devil in the form of a black dog. The legend of the Black Dog of Bungay (now locally referred to as Bob) is depicted on a fork of lightning on the top of an electric light standard near the Butter Cross, the awesome event being recorded on a plate at the base with the rhyme:

> All down the church in midst of fire
>   The hellish monster flew;
> And passing onwards to the Quire
>   He many people slew.

Most of Bungay was destroyed in a great fire in 1688, and much of the architecture we see today is eighteenth-century. The Butter Cross, a domed octagonal shelter supported on pillared arches, must be one of the finest in East Anglia and replaced an earlier one after the fire.

The romantic centrepiece of the town is the castle, the ruined fortress of the Bigod family who built it between 1164 and 1294. Although little remains inside the castle wall, the wall itself is imposing, with its twin-towered gatehouse which now allows entry over the old drawbridge pit by way of a footbridge. The ruins are quietly tucked away in the centre of the town and set in a secluded green no more than a few steps from the busy streets.

Bungay also had a marine trade at one time. The head of navigation is now about four miles downstream at Geldeston Lock, which was closed in 1934. There is a mooring staithe here and a footbridge across the river, and the old lock-keeper's cottage now forms the centrepiece of the recently enlarged Locks Inn.

Bungay Castle

The Waveney Valley is such an ideal setting for a wildlife reserve that it is not surprising to find one dedicated to another threatened species – the otter. The Otter Trust at Earsham, near Bungay, was founded by Philip and Jeanne Wayre in 1972 with the principal objective of 'promoting the conservation of otters throughout the world with particular emphasis on the British otter'.

Like so much of the wildlife in recent years, otters have been affected by disturbance and pollution, and their numbers have declined in Broadland and on most other lowland rivers. They are shy and secretive creatures and, coupled with the loss of so much of their riverside territory, it is a rare occurrence to see them in their natural habitat.

The trust has been successful in reversing the tragic decline of the otter by breeding them in captivity for release into the field, and since this programme of reintroduction began in 1982, it has been found that those released or their progeny have been successfully breeding in the wild. With the government promoting the 'green' message and, hopefully, *acting* on it, and with industry beginning to clean up its own act and those responsible for recreational facilities conscious of environmental protection, the Wayres' achievement in restoring the otter to the wild in increasing numbers should ensure the survival of the species for future generations.

Regular surveys are carried out on wild otter populations and their habitats by the trust's scientific personnel, and during the last decade or so over 220 otters havens have been created throughout the rivers of East Anglia, protected through management agreements with the landowners concerned. The trust also has another reserve in the West Country.

The headquarters at Earsham are ideally situated along the northern bank of the river and cover the spacious otter pens, three lakes with a variety of waterfowl as well as geese and swans which freely come and go; riverside walks, marsh and meadows and a coppice where the muntjac deer roam at liberty, complete the lovely setting of this reserve, which presents another aspect of wildlife conservation in Broadland.

Motoring through Broadland offers such a choice of routes that a decision as to which to take is more difficult than choosing a course in a boat. Apart from the few main highways, there is such a variety of minor roads and lanes branching off to so many delightful places that it would be no surprise if objectives tend to be confusing.

Once across the river at Beccles, the main road north-east (A143) takes you through Haddiscoe and St Olaves (where you cross the Waveney again) and on past Fritton Lake to Yarmouth; about half-way between the two there is a turn-off through Belton village to Burgh Castle, where the Waveney merges with Breydon Water. For the northern region the central route (B1140) eventually brings you to Reedham Ferry on the Yare. This is the most interesting route, if only because of the quaint experience of taking the chain ferry – provided there is not a long tailback to join. The ferry is a vehicular platform with the chain gear driven by a diesel engine, and it is the only means of getting your car across the Yare between Norwich and Yarmouth. The ferry is a short distance upstream from Reedham village, which has a number of pubs and a couple of hotels; there is also a good hostelry at the ferry in which you can relax with a drink and watch the less relaxed helmsmen of the hire cruisers make their cautious approaches to the ferry.

North from Reedham is Acle, a small market town linked to the Bure via a dike; from here the choice is north-west to South Walsham, Ranworth and Wroxham or north-east to Potter Heigham, Hickling and Horsey. From Potter Heigham, west, you can also reach Wroxham via Ludham and Horning.

The lovely waterside villages now easily accessible by car once depended for their survival almost entirely on the rivers. Before the arrival of the railways and the motor road, practically everything and everyone was carried by water.

One of the early sailing-freighters was the Norfolk keel. This was a single-masted, square-rigged vessel and when loaded was probably a cumbrous handful in the narrow waterways, although present knowledgeable opinion suggests that her overall performance was not so inefficient as generally supposed. Passengers travelled in light craft propelled by oarsmen, and these vessels were known as wherries. Some carried a small spritsail which gave them a better performance to windward than the square-sailed keel. From these light and manœuvrable craft evolved a cargo vessel with a hull shape and a rig that came closer to meeting the particular conditions of her home waters – the Norfolk trading wherry. After a long process of development, the wherry reached the peak of efficiency by the nineteenth century, when large fleets were trading between Yarmouth and Norwich and the many other towns and villages throughout the area. By this time she had replaced the keel.

'The Wherry,' Robert Malster writes in his comprehensive book *Wherries and Waterways,* 'was no bluff, unhandy barge. In general they were graceful and often beautiful vessels admirably suited to navigating the Norfolk and Suffolk waterways on which they developed.'

The wherry was certainly distinctive, with its low black hull, scarlet hatches and cabin top, and a stout mast forty feet high carrying one huge high-peaked sail. The black sail (dressed with tar and fish oil) was boomless and laced to a long gaff. The wherries were built of oak and were some fifty to sixty feet in length, with a draught of around four feet. They had a freight capacity of forty tons and carried a range of cargoes – timber, bricks, grain, flour, beer and a variety of other merchandise. Every village had its staithe, and wherries carried regular deliveries of coal to each from the collier brigs in Yarmouth harbour.

Apart from the fleets owned by some firms, many were owned by their skipper, who, with his mate or sometimes his wife, lived in the cosy but rather cramped cabin aft. They were easily handled by a crew of two. The mast was in a tabernacle but there was no standing rigging except for the stout forestay used for lowering and raising the mast, which was counterpoised by a heavy weight of iron or lead. The speed at which the mast could be lowered and raised was essential for 'shooting' bridges; as the wherry approached, mast and sail were dropped and as soon as the bridge was cleared were quickly raised again, the vessel having lost hardly any speed in the process. She was easy to tack, and with her sail set very flat and her hollow waterlines she performed well to windward. If there was little wind, man-power took over, with the quant, a twenty-four-foot spar with which the wherryman poled his craft along.

The heyday of the wherry was the nineteenth-century, and it was during the early part of this era that a group of Norwich businessmen, having become frustrated with the delays and increasing costs of trans-shipping goods at Yarmouth, decided to make the Yare navigable for sea-going vessels with an outlet to the sea at Lowestoft. Lowestoft men welcomed this opportunity to compete with Yarmouth, and a lock was built at Mutford Bridge at the eastern end of Oulton Broad, allowing passage into Lake Lothing and the harbour.

To avoid Breydon Water and save miles of navigation, a canal was dug from Haddiscoe to Reedham, joining the Waveney with the Yare, and this straight stretch of water is known to Broads sailors as the New Cut. A channel was also dug through Oulton Dyke and Oulton Broad, and the waterway from Lowestoft to Norwich for sea-going vessels was eventually opened in 1833. But the new route was not a financial success: it was little used and the coming of the railways more or less sealed its fate. Meanwhile Yarmouth improved its own facilities and the channel through Breydon Water, and this route to Norwich for sea-going ships is still used by small freighters today.

It was the arrival of the railways and motor transport that also sealed the fate of the wherries, and although a few were still working under sail until the late 1930s, only one now remains – the *Albion*, owned by the Norfolk Wherry Trust.

· The trust was formed in 1949, with the aim of preserving at least one of these unique trading-craft working under sail. The *Albion*, built at Oulton Broad in 1898, was bought, restored and

Thatched boathouse, Oulton Dyke

re-rigged with a new mast and sail; she did, in fact, go back to
work again and with a full-time crew traded in the old way for
some three years. One of her cargoes in 1950 was building-
material for the renovation of the Berney Arms, once a
wherryman's pub, almost cut off except by water, and the first
secure mooring for Broads cruisers on the Yare just upstream of
Breydon Water. In spite of efforts by the trust, it soon became
evident that trading was no longer a viable proposition, and the
only way the *Albion* could earn her keep was by charter. This has
proved an enormous success, and from April to the end of
October each year, under the command of her skipper, she is busy
sailing her home waters with parties of enthusiasts who find that
helping to handle this sole suvivor of a once numerous fleet is a
rare and exciting experience.

The trust now has a permanent home for her, a floating berth
under cover on Womack Water off the Thurne near Ludham.
When we saw her there, she had all the appearance of an on-going
trader. She is fifty-eight feet in length, with a beam of fifteen feet
and a draught of four feet six inches; under her cargo hatches her
hold has been skilfully converted to provide living-quarters for
twelve passengers without marring her character. She made a
strange and enchanting picture in contrast with the glassfibre
motor craft that passed on the river a stone's throw from her
berth. No wonder John Perryman, chairman of the trust, had a
proud glint in his eye when he showed us aboard.

The wherry Albion

From the neat decks for'ard of her mast and tabernacle, to the tiny steering cockpit with its stout tiller aft of the skipper's cabin, the *Albion* looked every inch a working craft. Trust members have worked hard to preserve her as such, although it is now pleasure sailing that is responsible for her new working life.

'She is now earning her keep,' John Perryman told us. 'A decade and more ago even chartering didn't cover her costs. In the last few years I think the general interest and concern with conservation and the preservation of working examples of the skills and crafts of the past have created the increasing demand we have had from people from all walks of life to sail on the *Albion*. She has given them the holiday of a lifetime and pleasure to thousands of others who, but for the trust, would never have seen a wherry under sail.'

I mentioned Robert Malster's book and recalled that he had written: 'The era of the wherry was the era of the windmill. Both used windpower, and both grew to be things of beauty whose passing was regretted long after they had disappeared from the Broadland scene.'

John Perryman nodded, well aware of the quotation. 'Most of the old working mills are derelict now but what the Norfolk County Council has done in preserving the best of them, the trust has done, and will continue to do, for the wherry,' he said.

Down in the south-eastern corner of Broadland is another aspect of the preservation theme, a commercial enterprise promoting the traditional skills of what has been a declining art in recent years – the craftsmanship of the master-boatbuilder.

For the past eight years or so, the International Boatbuilding Training Centre, under its founder and managing director, John Elliot, has been teaching the skills of building in wood to an increasing number of students of both sexes from Britain and from various parts of the world, including Japan. The range of craft built here varies from beautifully finished clinker dinghies to large and impressive ocean-going sailing-yachts from the boards of well-known designers. The training courses are always oversubscribed, and the reputation of the centre is such that the order book is always full.

The introduction of plastics in the 1950s spawned the glassfibre boat, and the skills and craftsmanship of building in wood began to disappear in the factory-type production of craft in the new material. Traditional boatyards fell back on fitting-out and maintenance work, and most of the boatbuilding craftsmen went into the general building trade. In the last decade or so, glassfibre yachts have taken on a more traditional appearance, in that wood has been re-introduced for interior furnishings, as well as softening the plastic look of the exterior with varnished trimmings. In any event, for every new design in glassfibre, a wooden mould must be built first; with the increasing use of timber in their deck trim and interior and a notable tendency in the market of a swing-back to the traditional all-timber boat, there is again a demand for craftsmen that exceeds the supply. The centre regularly receives invitations from boatyards around the country inviting qualified students to apply for work.

This revival of an old working tradition is another plus for the conservationists, and it is a rare sight to pass the centre, on the north shore of Lake Lothing, Lowestoft's inner harbour, and catch a glimpse of up to a dozen traditional craft in the making.

Lake Lothing itself, with its variety of marine activity, provides an unusual sight too, seen from the path that takes you along this shore from Oulton Bridge Road. There is always something to see – shipbuilding, repair work, trawlers in dry dock, gas-rig supply vessels, cargo-carriers, container berths and small working craft pottering the placid surface of the tideway. The path, which fringes marine workshops and boatyards, leaves the shore close to a quayside industrial complex and passes over the railway before eventually reaching the town.

Lowestoft is a successful mixture of trades. The marine industry, fishing and holidays have made this town on the most easterly point of land in the British Isles into a thriving and exhilarating place. South Town mostly stimulates the holiday element, with its hotels and boarding-houses along the south front; but Lowestoft's industrial heart is around the harbour. Despite the commercial expansion in recent years and the further development planned for the port, fishing still plays a major role in the town's economy, with a strong force of deep-sea trawlers. Lowestoft has one of the best fish docks and at one time competed with Yarmouth for the abundant North Sea herring; since the herring fishery declined in the post-war years, it has become one of the leading ports in the white-fish industry, topping every other in the country for plaice.

Yarmouth, on the other hand, once the main centre of the herring fleets, no longer has a fishing industry. Since the mid 1960s, when the last boats left the scene, the revival of the port's prosperity began with the discovery of North Sea oil and gas, Yarmouth being the first base for operations. The fish wharf and the long quays where the fishing fleets were once a familiar sight now serve the rig supply vessels, ro-ro ferries and container ships.

Gas rig ship entering Great Yarmouth

The gaunt, skeleton-like structures of the gas rigs seen offshore are a reminder of how things have changed.

Like Lowestoft, Yarmouth is a mix of the marine and holiday industries, but with greater scope along its broad sea-front for the leisure and pleasure element than its southern neighbour. The Marine Parade overlooking broad, sandy beaches offers a wide variety of entertainment. A huge leisure complex houses amusements and all-weather sporting facilities to keep the bucket-and-spade fraternity contented on wet days. It is a boisterous, happy place, thronged all summer with holiday-makers and day-trippers, many in funny hats; and catering for them, all the standbys of such a popular resort – cafés, ice-cream stalls, chip shops, souvenir shops and amusement arcades.

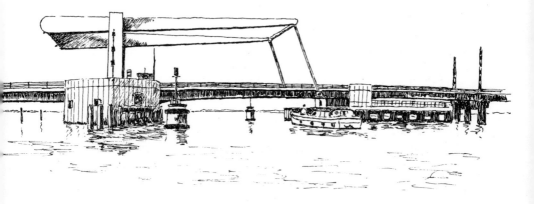

New bridge at Great Yarmouth, with Breydon Water beyond

The modern sea-front is a striking contrast to the old town, a bustling place at any time; but just west of the centre are North Quay and the Bure, an avenue of escape from the crowded streets. Just down the river and under the bridges is Breydon Water, the entrance to another world, a lonely Seago landscape of water and marsh and windmills.

8

The North Norfolk Inlets

The windswept north Norfolk coast, with its tidal creeks and small harbours filtering its saltmarshes and sand-dunes, is a wild and beautiful area of country, a landscape and seascape hard to match in any other part of East Anglia – or, indeed, England. It runs almost thirty miles east and west, edging the sea with shallow, wooded slopes rising behind coastal villages with names that seem to echo the character of their setting – Salthouse, Cley (pronounced Cly), Blakeney, Morston and Stiffkey, to name a few.

This coastline, from the village of Weybourne in the east to Old Hunstanton in the West, is an isolated world where Nature holds the stage immune from the threat of man, for almost the whole of this remote landscape of saltmarsh, mudflats, creeks and dunes is a succession of nature reserves.

It is as well that, long before the post-war expansion and the free reign of the developer, the claim to this land was staked by those organizations whose sole objective was to maintain and manage this natural heritage in perpetuity.

The National Trust and the RSPB, together with the Norfolk Naturalists Trust and other local organizations, own or manage much of this lovely coastline, which the Countryside Commission, with the support and encouragement of the Norfolk County Council, has designated a Heritage Coast and an Area of Outstanding Beauty.

One of the best introductions to the area is the approach from Weybourne in the east, where the cliffs of Sheringham end and the marshes begin. The road to Salthouse and Cley is one of the loveliest stretches along this coast and before reaching the low level of the marshes sets the scene for what lies ahead.

Salthouse is the most easterly of the coastal villages, a small, delightful huddle of flint pebble houses and fishermen's cottages, some of them now serving as holiday homes for distant townsfolk. It lies back from the road skirting the marsh to nestle against the gentle slope of the fields, and this prominence of arable or wooded land rising from the coast road for much of the way forms an attractive backdrop to many of the coastal villages. Another typical feature is the architectural style: Salthouse, like the others, is a 'flint village', for flint is used in the building of most of the houses, which, with their weathered pantiled roofs, make for a sense of harmony and style which is almost exclusive to this part of Norfolk.

The road runs west between marshes and field banks to Cley-next-the-Sea. Here the Salthouse and Cley marshes adjoin and form the Cley Nature Reserve. The visitors' centre is just outside the village, overlooking the reserve and the sea. The reserve covers 776 acres and provides eleven hides. There is a public footpath along the east bank, and a public road to the beach, with a car-park just below the shingle embankment. It is a haven for a wide variety of resident and migrating birds, and the wildfowl in winter include several thousand brent-geese and widgeon. Cley has the distinction of being the oldest county trust nature reserve in Britain and was purchased by the Norfolk Naturalists Trust in 1926, at the time the organization was founded.

Cley's most prominent feature is the beautifully preserved eighteenth-century tower windmill, probably the most popular subject along this coast with artists and photographers. It stands on the old quay overlooking the marshes and the River Glaven, but with a foreground of reed-beds so dense that the winding course of the river is almost lost from view.

This is another lovely village, its narrow main street twisting between old flint-built houses. The eighteenth-century Custom House reminds you that Cley was once a port and, like Blakeney next door, had a thriving trade with the Continent. The influence of the Dutch is notable in some of the buildings, which gives the place something of a Continental atmosphere. The church is another reminder of Cley's early prosperity, for it was rebuilt and enlarged when the maritime trade was at its peak.

Over the river bridge, up the hill and high on the edge of Blakeney village is the church. Its great west tower over a hundred

Cley Mill

feet high, dominates the landscape; but its most unusual feature is the slender east tower, which is said to have served as a beacon for ships entering Blakeney harbour.

A famous name in the churchyard is that of Sir Henry 'Tim' Birkin, one of Britain's most notable racing drivers, who died in 1953. He raced at Brooklands in the late 1920s and early thirties, driving Bentleys, and his successes on the track obviously played their part in establishing the Bentley as one of the finest sports cars in the world. Blakeney must have held a special charm for him, for he was a frequent visitor, although he never lived there.

Blakeney could not fail to charm any visitor. It is perhaps the most delightful village along this coast – and they are all attractive. It is still a small port but now concentrates on holidays and sailing, which long ago replaced its maritime commerce. Despite its popularity, it remains unspoilt. Flanking its narrow High Street, which runs down to the quay, are lovely old merchants' houses and fishermen's cottages which have been carefully converted into shops and holiday homes. New residential development which has appeared in recent years has been suitably controlled in location and design, so that it does not spoil the carefully preserved character of the old village.

There are two good hotels, one dominating the quay and the other nearby, overlooking an open duck pool and the marshes. From the quay the long channel, which drains at low tide, runs down between marsh and shingle bank to the harbour known as

Blakeney

'The Pit', protected by Blakeney Point, a nature reserve owned by the National Trust.

The point is a lonely, windswept place, a shingle spit on which huge sand-dunes have built up, stabilized by a mixture of vegetation. It has been a nature reserve since 1912 and a mecca for bird-watchers and botanists. It is one of the more important nesting-sites for terns; oystercatchers and other familiar waders are there in large numbers, and several rare species of migrating birds appear in the spring and autumn. From the dune heights the view, compass-round, takes in sea and shingle, sands and mudflats, marshes and creeks – a wild, impressive panorama lit with the changing shades of light and colour characteristic of this fascinating coast.

There are a number of hides, and an information centre within the strange shape of the old lifeboat house nestling amid the dunes. The reserve is open all year, and there is no charge to the public. Joe Reed, the head warden, and his assistants are always ready to advise and answer questions.

Blakeney Point can be reached via a three-mile shoreline walk from Cley, although most visitors arrive by boat from Blakeney Quay or from the creek at Morston, the next village. A small fleet of open motorboats operated by private boatmen takes visitors to the point, not only to observe the birds but also to see the seals, for at Blakeney there has always been a large colony of common seals which can be seen in the water or hauled out on the sands west of the point.

Like those in the Wash and elsewhere, the colony at Blakeney was tragically decimated by the North Sea sea virus which began in the late summer of 1988. Many organizations were involved in the work of rescue and research, including the National Trust, the Sea Mammal Research Unit in Cambridge and the RSPCA, which, with Greenpeace, set up the Seal Assessment Centre at Docking in north-west Norfolk. A tagging programme was introduced to help monitor the movements of both sick and healthy animals in the wild, and many samples were taken from dead seals in order to trace the origins of the virus and to find out whether pollution had in some measure been responsible.

Joe Reed and his assistants were heavily involved at Blakeney, working with others in the rescue and tagging and having the distressing job of burying many carcases.

'It was a sad and gruesome task,' Joe Reed recalls. 'A summer we'd never wish to see again. From a former colony of 750 seals, only 250 remained.'

Old lifeboat house, Blakeney Point

Seals off Blakeney Point

Altogether over 4,000 dead seals were found around the British coast, most of them on the beaches of Norfolk and the Lincolnshire shores of the Wash. By the beginning of 1989 it seemed the disease had declined, and through the summer and up to the time of writing (winter 1989–90) there has been little sign of the virus; but scientific research continues, as there is always a possibility that it could reappear.

Apart from this disastrous event, there has always been a need for the rescue of orphan and ailing pups, a number of which are found each year. Usually these abandoned youngsters are emaciated creatures too helpless to fend for themselves and the voluntary rescue services, some operating long before the epidemic, continue their life-saving task. Once the pups are restored to health and able to survive on their own, they are returned to the wild.

Media coverage of the disaster brought the plight of the seals dramatically to the attention of the public, some of whom were probably unaware that seals even existed around Britain's coasts, let alone having any knowledge of the rescue services. Public sympathy was aroused, many gave their support in time and money to the rescue and research operations, and a keen interest generally in the welfare of this fascinating animal has now increased enormously. This was evident when I was last at Blakeney. Although the seals here were a popular attraction with visitors before the media spotlight was centred on them, there seemed to be more boats crammed with more visitors (many wearing 'Save the Seal' T-shirts) off the seal sand than I have observed on previous occasions, and this was at the end of the autumn holiday season.

A mile or so west is Morston, where the church, on a rise overlooking the road, signifies the entrance to the village, a small community where boats and the holiday trade are a major part of its lifestyle. The pub stands at the centre, where the lane runs down to Morston Creek, another popular embarkation place for Blakeney Point and the seals.

Common seal

About a couple of miles south of Morston is Langham, typical of many of the other quiet inland villages but particularly interesting because it is the home of another traditional craft. The old buildings and converted Norfolk barn, pantiled and flint-faced, give no indication of the activity inside, where a team of craftsmen work with molten glass using blowing-irons and hand tools in the same way as glassmakers have for centuries. Langham Glass House is open to visitors and can claim that it is probably the only one in the country 'making glass commercially in any reasonable quantity, completely by hand'. Their descriptive little guide goes on: 'This is not just because we want to keep alive an ancient craft but also because it is frequently the only way of making a piece of glass that can no longer be made by any other means.' To study the process of this ancient craft and watch the glass-blowers at work is well worth the detour from the coast road.

Just west of Morston is Stiffkey, another charming flint village where the coast road is squeezed into a narrow street that runs right through it. The River Stiffkey runs at the back of the village and reveals its presence occasionally between the buildings overlooking the little valley. The community is served by a village store but, surprisingly, there is no village pub. Stiffkey was once well known for its 'Stewky Blues', a particular type of cockle gathered by hand at low water; but it is perhaps more likely to be remembered for its pre-war rector, the Revd Harold Davidson, who in the early 1930s switched the spotlight on himself and the village by his association with London women, most of whom were, to put it mildly, of loose character. Whether or not there was any truth in his excuse that he was trying to reform them, he was eventually defrocked and became a pathetic figure, spending the last years of his life as a music-hall turn.

The most interesting part of Wells-next-the-Sea is the waterfront, although the sea is more than a mile away at high tide and twice as far at low water. Despite the difficult entrance, drying sands and long, narrow tidal channel running up to the quay, Wells is a thriving little port and the only one of the north Norfolk harbours that retains a maritime trade. This has grown considerably in recent years and covers mainly animal feedstuffs, fertilizer, timber and other farm products. Coasters are now almost an everyday sight alongside the quay; in fact, around 200 small freighters use the port each year, in addition to the fishing fleets which are now concerned mainly with the whelk trade. The variety of working and pleasure craft to be seen off the quay and moored in the tidal creeks dazzle the eye with their colourful forms, and the creeks themselves winding through the saltmarshes appear as watery avenues of mystery waiting to be explored.

Apart from residential and light industrial development, Wells retains its old seaport character, with picturesque narrow streets and yards running back from the waterfront, although along the quay some fine old buildings have been altered to accommodate cafés and amusements catering for the modern holiday-maker. Many of these are housed in the big holiday caravan park located near the beach, almost a mile from the quay. A road behind the channel wall serves the site and a public car-park, which are separated from the sand dunes by a long belt of pines. On a shingle point at the end of the harbour channel is the lifeboat station, and from here, where the dunes roll back to merge with the flat, sandy shoreline fronting the tree belt, Holkham Bay opens out in all its breathtaking magnitude. In certain conditions, walking this beach at low tide, the strange, empty loneliness of the sands, with the tall, dark pines shadowing the dunes, creates almost a foreboding atmosphere – the ideal setting for one of M.R. James' Norfolk ghost stories.

Wells-next-the-Sea

Needless to say, you are in a nature reserve, and as an alternative to walking the beach there is a path through the woodland which takes you to Holkham Gap and the main entrance to the bay. From the pines a lane links the beach with the coast road opposite the entrance to Holkham Hall, a great eighteenth-century country house in the classical style. Built by the wealthy Coke family, the magnificent house and extensive park are open to the public at certain times during the season.

Holkham National Nature Reserve is the largest in England and Wales, a beautiful haven of sand-dune, saltmarsh, creeks, woodland and reclaimed agricultural land, rich in a variety of flora and fauna. The reserve covers the coastal area between

Blakeney in the east and Burnham Overy in the west and is managed by the Nature Conservancy Council in co-operation with the Holkham Estate.

The coast road west twists and undulates with many glimpses of the sea, the sand-dunes and tiny, half-hidden creeks filtering the marshes. After a few miles of this pretty route you are in the neighbourhood of the Burnhams, a group of seven villages which carry the same prefix to their names since they lie in the vicinity of the little River Burn.

Burnham Thorpe, small, quiet and tucked away in the Burn valley, is famous as the birthplace of Horatio Nelson. Apart from the pub (Lord Nelson) there is little in the village to denote that it has such an eminent association with the naval hero. The church, on the other hand, does house a graphic display of Nelson memorabilia, highlighting some of the famous events in the admiral's life as well as those less well known; and the white ensign is sometimes flown from the church tower.

Nelson was born in 1758 at the rectory (his father was rector), and from an early age his interest in the sea drew him to walk the coast nearby and to study the fishing-craft and trading-schooners at the port of Wells. No doubt he first learned to sail on the sheltered local waters of Overy Staithe and Brancaster; he left his last school to join the Navy when he was thirteen. Although his enthusiasm for the sea was paramount, he loved the countryside of his birth and was proud to be a Norfolk man. The old rectory was demolished after his father died in 1802, three years before the death of his illustrious son, and the present house was built on the site.

Burnham Thorpe is the most southerly of the Burnhams. Just north-west of it is Burnham Market, which has a prosperous, uncluttered air about it, with its broad main street and tree-shaded green overlooked by some lovely Georgian houses. Up on the coast road Burnham Overy is rather scattered but nonetheless very charming. Its proudest feature must be the splendid windmill standing high above the River Burn and, just below it, the old watermill with its cluster of cottages grouped by the riverside, a tranquil picture no artist should miss.

Burnham Overy Staithe is another on my list of favourite waterside villages. It has a pub called 'The Hero' (a number of pub signs in the area are a reminder that you are in Nelson country) and is one of the prettiest of the Burnhams, particularly down by the quay, where a terrace or two of picturesque cottages overlook the creek and the hard. On the ebb and flow of the tide the little harbour is alive with small boats. Across the saltings and creeks is

Scolt Head Island, a nature reserve owned jointly by the National Trust and the Norfolk Naturalists Trust and leased to the Nature Conservancy Council; but there is a better view of it from Brancaster Staithe, a little further west. In between are Burnham Norton and Burnham Deepdale, the most westerly of the Burnhams.

Burnham Overy Staithe

The straight village street cuts through the centre of Brancaster Staithe, with vehicle access to the waterside at the far end. Here there is a very active sailing club fronting a spacious hard that shelves into the mud at low water but gives you a clean embarkation area if you are stepping into a dinghy when the tide serves. Brancaster harbour is not only large and dotted with boats but also conveniently sheltered by Scolt Head Island. Like all the inlets along this coast, it dries out at low water but on a rising tide the sea is in easy reach of the sailor, the channel running out between the west point of the island and Brancaster beach. If you don't want to go to sea, you can take the tide in a small boat and sail between the island and the saltings round to Overy Staithe.

Scolt Head is a wild and lonely place that will remind you of Blakeney Point, but when you are there you seem to feel its isolation even more, because it is an island. It is four miles long and about a mile across at its broadest point and is formed of sand dunes on a base of shingle. The seaward shoreline is predominantly shingle and sand, with saltmarshes, shingle and mudflats to the south. Over the years the dunes at the centre have built up into enormous sand-hills stabilized by vegetation, one rising to a height of a hundred feet.

Brancaster Staithe

Apart from the rich variety of animal and plant life of interest to botanists and ornithologists, the island's changing configuration over the years, due to reworking by the sea of sand and shingle, provides a continuing study for physical geographers and biologists. National Trust warden Richard Lowe explained this when we landed at the western end of the island, and by taking an old wreck as a marker it was possible to illustrate the progressive westward growth caused by this movement of sand and shingle.

We left the tideline and moved through the marram grass across the island towards the sea. Scolt Head is noted particularly for its large ternery, located at the western end, but as I was there in the autumn, these summer visitors had long since gone. However, I saw a number of residents – oystercatchers, redshanks, ducks and many of the winter arrivals, including widgeon and brent- and pink-footed geese. Seals are frequently seen off shore, and although there is no breeding colony there, some seventy dead and dying animals were washed up on the beaches of Scolt Head and Brancaster during the epidemic.

As we walked the deserted shoreline where the sea had pushed the shingle into ridges towards the dunes, I found that even here the high tideline had its share of litter common to many stretches of the sea and estuary shores in the south – empty beer cans, plastic containers, bottles and broken boxes, an offensive display washed up by the tide, typical of this throw-away age. Clearing this regular supply of litter is the frustrating task of the wardens and their assistants. Not such a tragic and gruesome job as dealing with the result of the seal virus, but one visible aspect of pollution. I wondered if there were any others, such as oil. I put the thought to Richard.

'There has been the occasional oiled sea-bird,' he said, 'but no oil on the beaches. Of course, some pollution you can't detect until you test the water; mussels are a good indicator here, as they show up the first signs. There are a number of mussel lays in the harbour, and samples are regularly taken from these for analysis.'

As we paused for breath on a high dune, my companion indicated with a sweep of his arm the land and waterscape around us, silent but for the calls of the waders.

'Have you thought,' he asked, 'what might have happened to all this – and other such places – if it had not been for the conservationists? Protection of these areas benefits not only the wildlife but the public too, since they are free to enjoy the beauty, whether their pleasure is sailing, fishing, observing or just walking. Conservation means retaining the essential character of a beautiful area or a property and yet making it accessible to everyone.'

This applies to Scolt Island, of course. During the summer, by prior arrangement, the local boatmen at Brancaster Staithe will ferry you across; the trip can usually be made two or three hours either side of high water.

I asked Richard if he ever came over in summer when he was off-duty and could be somewhere else. He nodded, and I was reminded of a similar question I had put to Charles Underwood at Orfordness. As we moved down the shore to the boat, I received a similar answer.

'What could be better,' Richard said, 'than a deserted beach like this for a picnic and a swim?'

Richard Lowe is not likely to change his lifestyle – and who would blame him!

Less than a couple of miles separate Brancaster from Brancaster Staithe, and in between the two, on Rack Hill, is the site of the Roman fort of Branodunum, from which the name Brancaster is said to have derived. Although some residential development on the outskirts gives the approaches a modern look, the village centre is still very much in character with its neighbours. A lane, subject to flooding, leads down to the clubhouse and golf course on the seaward side of the saltings and to Brancaster beach.

Titchwell, almost adjoining Brancaster, consists of no more than a few houses, a round-towered church and two very good inns, but it is especially noted for its fine RSPB reserve. This is a 420-acre site extending from just north of the road, its seaward boundary skirting the shore. The reserve has a mixture of habitats, including fen and woodland, marshes, reedbeds and a tidal creek. Walking the path along the western boundary to the dunes is a rewarding experience, and even if you are not a keen ornithologist, you cannot fail to be enchanted by the natural beauty of this wildlife haven. The reserve centre, near the car-park, is open during the summer, and access is free throughout the year.

Thornham is next, the last little harbour along this coast. Neat houses and cottages, of brick and stone and some of flint, spread from the main street towards the marshes. Thornham harbour, like the others we have seen, was once a busy port, but now all that remains is a muddy tidal creek surrounded by marshes, with here and there a boat or two to remind you that the waterway is still in use.

The Thornham channel marks the eastern boundary of another lovely reserve. Holme Dunes, for which the Norfolk Naturalists Trust is responsible. A variety of habitats within its 550 acres takes in sand dunes, saltmarsh, grazing marsh, brackish and fresh-water lagoons, with a pine belt on part of the old dunes. Such a mixed composition harbours a range of small animals and a wealth of plant life, and amongst the great variety of birds are many rare species. It has a good location on the north-west corner of Norfolk, where the coast turns south to front the sand-strewn waters of the Wash, and with its different habitats the reserve is a convenient stop-over for passage migrants; it attracts numerous winter visitors and has a large resident population. In all, over 285 species have been recorded. You could spend days here walking the nature trails, the dunes and the shingle from the ragged marsh of Thornham channel to Lavender Marsh on the western boundary. With the golf course nearby and Holme-next-the Sea so close to the popular holiday resort of Hunstanton, this area is a crowded place in summer.

Holme is where the Peddars Way, running up through west Norfolk from the Suffolk border, joins the Norfolk Coast Path, running west to Cromer; in all a ninety-three-mile route through a contrasting vista of beautiful country. But the coastal path is my choice. It will appeal to all those ramblers who prefer the scents of the marshes and the nearness of the sea coupled with the isolation and the wildlife and the colours that only this remote territory can give. It is, for so much of the way, a walk on the wild side.

9

The Wash to Denver

The low-lying coast from Hunstanton to King's Lynn runs south, flanking the eastern shore of the Wash, offering the Norfolk visitor an impressive introduction to this huge, strange arm of the sea. It can be a bleak coastline, with miles of sand exposed at low water and with hardly a break in its bold contour until it bulges outward to soften into a stretch of tidal marshes before reaching the east bank of the entrance to the Great Ouse, Lynn's maritime highway.

The sands are an extraordinary and fascinating feature within the basin-like contours of the Wash. At low water there is little but sand to be seen, except along so much of the Lincolnshire shore where the sand-flats are separated from the sea-wall by the broad green ribbon of the saltings, pierced here and there by muddy gutways that fill on the tide.

The shape of the sands and the direction of the channels are frequently changing. The present deep-water channel to King's Lynn is about two miles east of the old channel. This change took place in 1980 after an earlier change only nine years before. The tides run fast, and the tidal range is dramatic: a rise of up to twenty-two feet at King's Lynn and as high as twenty-six feet in the Wash itself.

To be out on the sands on a fine summer's day is a singular experience. Distant objects ashore or even a figure across the sands, shimmering in the haze, give a mirage-like impression. In clear weather you can see for miles: Hunstanton cliffs to the east and the church tower landmark of Boston Stump in the west, while the outer banks, cut by fast-flowing channels, break the seascape view into desert islands here and there shadowed by basking seals.

The long shore sands, tempting though they may be, are not for the inexperienced explorer. Firm and dry after the tide has receded, they tend to give a false impression of security. The tide goes out a long way and comes back quickly, and long, twisting gullies dry to cross on your way seaward become fast-flowing creeks that may cut off your return.

The sands have intriguing names – Old South, Gat, Toft, Friskney Flat, Blackguard, Thief and Seal are some, the latter, perhaps, being the most appropriate of all, for the Wash has the largest population of common seals in Britain.

The common seals' environment is essentially the shallow seas, and the shoal waters of the East Anglian coast and estuaries where sand and mud-banks appear on the out-going tide are where the common seals are found. They are hardy animals, the male having a life span of around twenty years and the female thirty years. When they dive, their body functions slow down and they can remain submerged for up to forty minutes, even sleeping under water, floating to the surface to breathe without waking. They have good hearing, and their sight is better in water than on land. The pups are born in June and July and weigh up to twenty-five pounds at birth. With their round, dog-like heads, lovely dark eyes and long whiskers, so essential to their sense of touch, they have an endearing appearance when they appear above the surface. Their caterpillar-like movement when they haul out is in stark contrast to their symmetrical performance in the water, where they can attain a speed of up to fifteen miles per hour. They live on a diet of fish, including shellfish, and at low water spend much of their time hauled out, sleeping or yawning, scratching or just basking in the sun.

Their characteristic of hauling out on those tidal banks close to a deep water channel or the sea, into which they can plunge at the first sign of disturbance, is adequately catered for in the Wash, and it is no surprise that this area, which has more of these facilities than any other, supports so many colonies. What perhaps is surprising is the size of the population, which has for many years numbered between six and 7,000, to which can be added a small colony of grey seals. Needless to say, the tragic seal disease of 1988 hit this area the hardest, and the numbers were drastically reduced.

Sheila Anderson of the Sea Mammal Research Unit at Cambridge tells me that a survey conducted after the epidemic revealed that fifty per cent of the former population has been lost. Although there is no certainty that the disease will not recur, the conservation of the remaining colonies seems promising, since most of the adult seals now appear to have assumed an immunity. The danger is in summer, during two periods when large groups gather and any infection is easily transmitted – that is, at the time of the pupping season, when the young are susceptible to any risk, as is any newly born creature, and three or four weeks later, when seals begin a period of moult.

The Sea Mammal Research Unit works closely with the other organizations concerned, an important one of which is the Seal Assessment Unit at Docking, now run entirely by the RSPCA under the direction of Dr Sue Mayer. The unit is really a seal hospital, set up after the outbreak of the disease. Its facilities include a post-mortem room, isolation pens with accommodation for up to fourteen seals, ten intermediate pools to which seals are moved when they are capable of feeding themselves, and five deeper pools for their final rehabilitation.

Here, round-the-clock care by a dedicated nursing team has resulted in the return to the wild of many seals that would have died, and when I was there (autumn 1989), Dr Mayer told me that, since the unit was established, 134 seals had been treated. Although a large number of these had died, the majority from the virus, forty-nine had been released, two being returned to the wild at Blakeney while I was there. A week or so before my visit, a hooded seal pup, a vagrant from Icelandic waters, had been found on a Suffolk beach, restored to health at the unit and air-lifted for release in the Shetlands, the nearest point to his home environment.

I asked Dr Mayer if any of their recent patients had shown any sign of the disease.

'Thankfully none, not since the spring,' she said. 'Our work since then has centred mainly around the rearing of pups separated from their mothers. Normally these pups would die of starvation and injuries sustained as they wander about in search of their parent.'

Although these strays showed no sign of the virus infection, neither was there any evidence of significant immunity to the disease, and an important part of the work is to vaccinate the animals and monitor their response to the vaccination, ensuring their protection when returned to the sea. The unit also assists in research projects that monitor the health, immune status and pollution levels in seals.

The unit's work in rehabilitation must begin to compensate for the loss of so many seals in the Wash and surrounding areas, and I put this point to Dr Mayer.

'It should make a positive contribution to repopulation,' she said. 'But constant monitoring will be needed in future.'

The unit at Docking is strategically placed roughly equidistant between the Wash and the north-west Norfolk coast. Another seal rescue service appropriately sited is at King's Lynn.

West Norfolk Seal Rescue is a well-known voluntary service, founded and run by Mr and Mrs Giles from their home on the outskirts of the town. Their garden is a seal sanctuary with two pools, isolation pens and the other necessary facilities. Much has been written and filmed about them, particularly during the epidemic, when they worked day and night coping with up to forty seals at any one time. The epidemic has abated, hopefully never to recur, but the rescue work goes on, as it did before, and at the time of writing they have twenty seals in their care. It is a continuous life-saving task to which they devote all their time, and since they began fourteen years ago, 260 seals have been returned to the wild.

King's Lynn, more often referred to locally as Lynn, is large and prosperous, its fortunes as a sea-port and market town going back into the Middle Ages. Its expansion in recent years has been rapid, with new roads and industrial estates mainly in its southern outlying districts. A large shopping precinct built in the 1960s has modernized a part of the old centre of the town, but once out of this you are back in Lynn's medieval period, reflected in its narrow streets and many fine buildings, for whose preservation much is owed to King's Lynn Civic Society and the King's Lynn Preservation Trust.

Some of the very best of period architecture can be found on or near the waterfront. Here, along the quays and amidst the old merchants' houses, a sense of the past conjures up a picture of Lynn's history and early maritime trade. The centuries of sail, when the river and the wharves were packed with square-riggers and schooners, generated the great periods of Lynn's prosperity. Trade routes to the Baltic, the Low Countries, the Mediterranean and later America were opened up. Trading links were established with the Hanseatic League, an influential association of north European merchants, founded in the fifteenth century, who recognized Lynn's importance. Agriculture too played its part, with a wealth of produce from the farmlands to the west and the south, combining the port with a successful market town.

Defoe, on his eighteenth-century journey, found Lynn a 'rich and populous thriving port-town'. He observed that 'they bring in more coals than any port between London and Newcastle, and import more wines than any port in England except London and

Bristol.' He also found it a very lively town: 'Here are more gentry and consequently more gaiety in this town than in Yarmouth, or even Norwich itself, the place abounding in very good company.'

Much of this good company was wealthy company that left a legacy of period buildings, beautifully preserved, to feast the eye, and probably there is no better place to begin the feast than Tuesday Market Place. Lying close to Common Staithe Quay, it is certainly one of the best market squares in Norfolk. It is flanked by many attractive houses, mostly Georgian and Victorian, and includes the eighteenth-century Corn Hall. Two or three good hotels overlook this great open space, which is thronged with stalls and people on market day and serves as a car-park at other times. The Duke's Head presents one of the best fronts, dating from 1689 and designed by a local architect, Henry Bell, who was responsible for several of the architectural gems the town takes pride in preserving.

Following the river up and within not much more than a stone's throw from it are King Street and Queen Street, and for practically all the way there is nothing of the modern trend to disturb their

Old buildings, King's Lynn

character. St George's Guildhall at the start of King Street is early fifteenth-century and is the largest and oldest hall of a merchant guild remaining in the country. It was a theatre in Shakespeare's time and since then has been used as a warehouse, courthouse and armoury. It is now an arts centre, with a theatre, galleries and restaurant, and is the headquarters of the King's Lynn Festival in July each year.

At the end of King Street is the Custom House, the only complete example of Bell's work that remains in the town. This impressive stone building on Purfleet Quay was erected in 1683 as the Merchants' Exchange and became the Custom House in 1718. The splendid eighteenth-century front of Clifton House in Queen Street has an eye-catching portico with twisted columns. Behind it is a five-storey Elizabethan watchtower, and recent restoration work has brought to light two early fourteenth-century tiled floors. The house is thought to have been renovated by Bell around 1708. Further along is Thoresby College, originally built about 1500 to house the priests of the Trinity Guild, but what remains now is mostly from the seventeenth-century.

Saturday Market Place is dominated by St Margaret's Church, which presents a striking picture of periods and styles, some parts of the building dating back to the twelfth century. It went through many early phases of change and rebuilding: in the fifteenth century the poor foundations gave way under the north-west tower, and a new one was built in the Perpendicular style, but the extraordinary angle of the original tower can still be seen inside. The church's spacious interior contains some splendid finely carved screens, and in the south chancel aisle are two of the largest brasses in England. Another unusual gem is the seventeenth-century moon clock which tells the time of high water. Outside, as if relating to this, on the lower parts of the west doorway are a number of marks recording the different levels reached by the floodwaters at various times, including the inundation of 1953.

Despite the imposing presence of the church, the first building in Saturday Market Place to focus your attention must surely be the Guildhall. It has a magnificent façade presenting a bold, chequered pattern in flint and freestone. Behind the main hall are two large rooms, one an assembly hall and the other a card room built in 1767; it is now part of the town hall. Amongst the corporation's treasured regalia are the gold and enamelled 'King John's Cup' and 'King John's Sword' – although they both bear his name, it is known that they are of a later period. However, King John had a close relationship with Lynn, having giving it its first charter in 1205; but he is perhaps best remembered for his

Custom House, King's Lynn

journey from Lynn to Newark in 1216, when he lost his baggage train in the Wash.

A wealth of medieval buildings is located in this quarter near the river – the Hanseatic warehouses flanking St Margaret's Lane and extending to South Quay, Hampton Court nearby, and not far away in Bridge Street the Greenland Fishery, dating from 1605, which became an inn during the eighteenth century much used by whalers. Wandering amongst these well-preserved architectural gems here and in other parts of the town, you tend to forget that Lynn is a modern industrial place and a highly successful port.

The docks are just north of Tuesday Market Place, beyond timber-yards and warehouses. When you see the port estate now, it is surprising to learn that the docks were built more than a century ago. Alexandra Dock was opened in 1869, and Bentinck Dock dates from 1883. The modern complex surrounding them is typical of the highly efficient port of today, with ro-ro, bulk and container facilities handling a range of cargoes – oil, chemicals, timber, grain and other products. Well over 1¼ million tons of freight pass through the port annually.

Always a fishermen's port, Lynn has a fishing industry which has expanded in recent years. Although catches include some white fish, shellfish and shrimps are the mainstay – Lynn whelks are now an established delicacy in Japan. The Fisher Fleet, a tidal inlet now within the port estate, its head reaching up between the two docks, has been the base for local fishermen since long before the docks were built. Fisher Fleet is a narrow, straight creek opening onto the river just downstream of the docks' entrance, and at low tide becomes a steep, mud-banked gutway with a variety of working craft sitting on the bottom. Here are wooden smacks and small shrimpers huddled amongst the powerful steel hulls of their modern counterparts. From the quay this closely packed fleet presents a confusing picture, a complex web of masts, ropes, rigging, derricks and gantries, stirring an atmosphere pervaded with the scent of mussels and cockles, whelks and shrimps, all the flavour of the sands and channels of the Wash.

The eleven-mile approach channel to the port is marked by light buoys and beacons, whose maintenance is the responsibility of the King's Lynn Conservancy Board. Ships up to 3,000 tons use the port, and the channel is navigable only around high water. Water depths are subject to change and are monitored by frequent and regular surveys. Buoy movements and maintenance of navigation marks and moorings are undertaken by the board's eighty-foot steel buoying vessel, which has an official title and number but is more affectionately known to the crew as 'the harbour master's barge'. I well remember her from many years ago, when I went aboard for an interesting day of buoy-changing operations, so it was a happy occasion when I was in Lynn again to walk into the harbour office and renew my acquaintance with Captain David Garside, who has been harbour master since 1968. We had an amusing interval recalling the voyage which had contributed so much to the background material I was researching for a book at the time (*Flip: The Story of a Seal*).

I remember we went down river soon after dawn on one tide and came back on the next, when the sun was low over the

King's Lynn dock area

fenland landscape. Lynn looks its most interesting from the river, and when we were coming up on the tide, the town and the waterfront bathed in the colours of the setting sun presented a picture reminiscent of a Dutch painting. For the artistic visitor, this Dutch-like impression of Lynn from the water is worth the ferryboat ride to West Lynn pier and can be appreciated even more in the broader view from the West Lynn bank of the river.

The Great Ouse is tidal up to Denver Sluice, near Downham Market, and still maintains a tidal strength to put off the leisurely inland-water sailor from nosing downstream of the sluice. Like most rivers in the marshland and the fens, it is enclosed within high banks, and at high tide the water is higher than the surrounding countryside for most of the way. Running parallel on its eastern side is the flood-relief channel, cut in the early 1960s to take the excess water from the fens into the sea via the head sluice at Denver and the tail sluice a mile or so upstream of the harbour at King's Lynn.

To turn off the main King's Lynn–Downham Market road (A10) at Watlington and drive to and over the river is to enter a strange country: a flat, endless landscape of drains and dikes, fields of green and fallow acres of dark rich soil, few boundary hedges or stone walls, nothing but a lonely farmhouse midst a cluster of trees, an isolated village pinpointed by its ancient church, to break the monotonous level of the land until it merges with the distant low horizon. And beyond that another horizon westward through the northern boundaries of Cambridgeshire into Lincolnshire, where the land provides an agricultural mix of arable farms, fruit farms and horticulture. To the south, amongst the rivers and water-courses, some of Britain's major wetland wildlife reserves have been established.

The Great Ouse to Denver borders the Norfolk marshland, and here are villages and churches dating back to the Middle Ages, all with evocative names that have a certain ring about them in relating to each other. The four Wiggenhalls, lying close to the river, are interesting examples. Just over the bridge from Watlington is the southernmost of the quartet, Wiggenhall St Mary Magdalen, typical of the small marshland villages; typically, too, it is the church that reflects the long history of these early settlements. It contains a number of interesting items of different periods, but the most noteworthy feature is the fifteenth-century glass in the north arcade. A mile or so down river on the other side, the church of Wiggenhall St Peter presents a stark picture of ruin, open to the sky and dominated by its tower hugging the river bank. In contrast, just north and on opposite sides of the Great Ouse, the churches of Wiggenhall St Germans and Wiggenhall St Mary the Virgin are noble buildings, each containing some striking medieval furnishings, of which the exquisitely carved fifteenth-century benches of St Mary the Virgin are the most outstanding.

The road just south of Wiggenhall St Magdalen hugs the base of the river embankment, and at Stowbridge you can cross the river again, cutting through Wimbotsham to Downham Market. Downham Market has spread a little, but its centre still retains the mellow charm of a small market town, with two small but comfortable hotels. The village of Denver, less than a mile away, has a superb corn-grinding windmill surrounded by grasslands and hedgerows, and once past the mill the clear approaches to the river open up, dominated by the gantry-like structures of the sluice.

Denver Sluice controls the outlet of water into the tidal Ouse and the sea from a drainage area of many hundreds of square miles. The first sluice was built by Vermuyden in 1651 as a tidal barrier, and this was followed eighty years later by the first navigation lock. The sluice was rebuilt in 1834 by John Rennie, when the old lock was replaced by the present one. The main change since then has been the replacement of the old timber doors with the two steel vertical lift gates.

Denver Sluice

From the sluice bridge the whole scene appears as a great water junction: up river the placid non-tidal waters of the Ouse, one arm of which branches into the relief channel; down the tidal stream is Salters Lode, its lock the entry to the Ouse–Nene navigation link, and just west of the bridge the long, straight cut of the New Bedford River, tidal as far up as Earith, spilling into the Great Ouse a few yards downstream of the sluice. Here is the beginning or the end (whichever way you are heading) of a vast inland waterway network, the holiday playground of so many pleasure-boat sailors and the haunt of so many bankside fishermen.

Denver is a fascinating place. Set in the same open countryside but protected by the grass-covered river walls and on the low east bank by a foliage spread of wild shrubs and trees, it has a pretty, haven-like charm about it. It is good walking-country, with a choice of inland pathways and breezy waterside banks to follow, and in summer the waters themselves are always a scene of activity. A variety of craft attracts the eye, from sailing dinghies to motor cruisers, and here and there the long, narrow hull of a canal boat. There is an active sailing club, and across the river opposite the club's headquarters is Jenyns Arms, a welcome hostelry with gardens running down to the waterside and nearby staithes conveniently placed for the mooring of boats with thirsty crews.

This piece of country, with its tidal link with the sea, is in sharp contrast to the marshes, inlets, estuaries and Broads embroidering the rest of the East Anglian coast. Each contrasting scene has its own enchantment, so much of it a natural world lying under the famous, and wide open East Anglian sky. Long may it remain so.

Glossary

Barrage	Artificial barrier in river equipped with large sluice-gates regulating the level or flow of water
Dike	Ditch or drain
Gaff	The spar to which the top of the sail is fitted
Groyne	Timber framework or broad concrete wall projecting into the water to prevent beach erosion and encroachment of the sea
Gun punt	Small flat-bottomed boat used by marshmen and wildfowlers for hunting
Gutway	Narrow waterway between mudbanks
Hard	Area at the edge of a river where gravel or other material has been laid to provide a firm surface
Keel	That part of a vessel projecting below the hull. In a sailing-craft the keel provides ballast and prevents the tendency to drift sideways due to wind pressure
Kissing-gate	Small gate hung in a U-shaped enclosure
Lighter	Flat-bottomed barge, usually towed, for transporting goods on rivers and in harbours; and for loading and unloading ships not brought to the wharf

Lugsail	Four-sided sail with the spar set at a wide angle to the mast
Maltings	Buildings in which barley or other grain is prepared for brewing or distilling
Mooring trot	Line of moorings. Tackle laid in such a way as to keep the boat floating in one position
Saltings	Saltmarsh
Sessions	An assembly for the transaction of legislative or judicial business
Shoal	Shallow; a shallow place
Staithe	Landing-stage or wharf
Postmill	A mill in which the body of the structure revolves on a central post, enabling the sails to capture a wind coming from any direction
Tidemill	Mill machinery operated by a water-wheel. A pool behind the mill traps the incoming tide; when the tide recedes the water in the pool is released and turns the wheel

Useful Addresses

Countryside Commission
Eastern Regional Office
Terrington House
13–15 Hills Road
Cambridge
CB2 1NL
Tel: Cambridge (0223)
354462

East Anglia Tourist Board
Toppesfield Hall
Hadleigh
Suffolk
IP7 5DN
Tel: Hadleigh (0473)
822922

The Essex Naturalists' Trust
Fingringhoe Wick Nature
Reserve
South Green Road
Fingringhoe
Colchester
Essex
CO5 7DN
Tel: Rowhedge (99128)
678

Field Studies Council
Flatford Mill Field Centre
East Bergholt
Colchester
Essex
CO7 6UL
Tel: Colchester (0206)
298283

Frinton & Walton Heritage Trust
7 South View Drive
Walton-on-the-Naze
Essex
CO14 8EP
Tel: Frinton (0255) 677087

The Harwich Society
4 Hall Lane
Harwich
Essex
CO12 3TE
Tel: Harwich (0255)
503429

King's Lynn Civic Society
23a Queen Street
King's Lynn
PE30 1HT
Tel: King's Lynn
(0553) 760085

King's Lynn Preservation Trust
Thoresby College
King's Lynn
PE30 1HX
Tel: King's Lynn (0553) 763871

National Trust
Eastern Regional Office
Blickling
Norwich
NR11 6NF
Tel: Aylsham (0263) 733471

Nature Conservancy Council
East Anglia Region
60 Bracondale
Norwich
NR1 2BE
Tel: Norwich (0603) 620558

Norfolk and Norwich Heritage Trust
Dragon Hall
115–23 King Street
Norwich
NR1 1QE
Tel: Norwich (0603) 663922

Norfolk Naturalists Trust
72 Cathedral Close
Norwich
NR1 4DF
Tel: Norwich (0603) 625540

Norfolk Wherry Trust
63 Whitehall Road
Norwich
NR1 3EN
Tel: Norwich (0603) 624642

The Otter Trust
Earsham
Nr Bungay
Suffolk
NR35 2AF
Tel: Bungay (0986) 3470

The River Stour Trust
1 School Cottage
Raydon
Ipswich
Suffolk
IP7 5LL
Tel: Ipswich (0473) 310807

Royal Society for the Protection of Birds
East Anglian Office
Aldwych House
Bethel Street
Norwich
NR2 1NR
Tel: Norwich (0603) 615920

Suffolk Wildlife Trust
Park Cottage
Saxmundham
Suffolk
IP17 1DQ
Tel: Saxmundham (0728) 3765

Bibliography

Many books have been written on East Anglia, including a number concerned only with the individual counties. Some cover the region in a general way, others a particular area or aspect of it. In the brief list below I have included only those titles to which I have referred in the text. Apart from the interest these books offer in themselves, many of them provide further reading on those places and subjects which in some instances I have only touched on in order to concentrate elsewhere.

In addition there are numerous local guides and publications such as those published by Jarrolds of Norwich, Poppyland Publishing of Norfolk, the series on the Suffolk coastal region by Jean and Stuart Bacon of Orford and the guide to Woodbridge by Carol and Michael Weaver. For the rambler the Ordnance Survey Pathfinder series, and on a more limited scale the footpath maps covering Essex and Suffolk published by Wilfrid George of Aldeburgh, save time in planning routes. These and other publications are usually available from local bookshops and stationers and from the information offices of the East Anglian Tourist Board in the areas concerned.

The National Trust, the county trusts, the RSPB, the Countryside Commission and other conservation bodies also publish detailed information on reserves: these are usually available at the various reserve reception centres.

Arnott, W.G., *Suffolk Estuary* (Norman Adlard, 1950)

Arnott, W.G., *Alde Estuary* (Norman Adlard, 1952)

Beardell, C.H., Dryden, R.C. and Holzer, T.J., *The Suffolk Estuaries* (Suffolk Wildlife Trust, 1988)

Benham, Hervey, *Down Tops'l* (Harrap, 1951)

Coote, Jack H., *East Coast Rivers* (*Yachting Monthly*; frequently revised editions)

Defoe, Daniel, *Tour Through the Eastern Counties* (East Anglian Magazine, 1949)

Edward, Russell, *The River Stour* (Terence Dalton, 1982)

Griffiths, Maurice, *The Magic of the Swatchways* (Edward Arnold, 1932)

Kinsey, Gordon, *Orfordness: Secret Site* (Terence Dalton, 1981)

Kinsey, Gordon, *Bawdsey: Birth of the Beam* (Terence Dalton, 1983)

Malster, Robert, *Wherries and Waterways* (Terence Dalton, 1971)

Malster, Robert, *Ipswich: Town on the Orwell* (Terence Dalton, 1978)

Pinney, Richard, *Smoked Salmon and Oysters* (Butley-Orford Oysterage, 1984)

Ransome, Arthur, *Secret Water* (Cape, 1939)

Roberts, Bob, *The Last of the Sailormen* (Routledge, 1960)

Roberts, Bob, *A Slice of Suffolk* (Terence Dalton, 1978)

Tennyson, Julian, *Suffolk Scene* (Blackie, 1939)

Yachting Guide to Harwich Harbour and Its Rivers (Harwich Haven Authority; annual publication)

Index

Page numbers in bold refer to illustrations.

Acle, Norfolk, 157
Adam, Robert, 52
Adnams brewery, 141
Albion (wherry), 158–61
Alde, river, 112, 122–9
Aldeburgh, Suffolk, 112, 125, 126–7
Aldeburgh Festival, 118, 124–5
Alderton, Suffolk, 103
Angel, Wally, 64
Ant, river, 145
Arnott, W.G., *Suffolk Estuary*, 86
  Alde Estuary, 116
Atomic Weapons Research Establishment, 120
avocets, 108

Bargate Water, 146
barge-racing, 73
Bawdsey, Suffolk, 103–5
Bawdsey Manor, 87–8, 103
Bawdsey Quay, 87, 103
Beaumont Creek, Essex, 17, 19
Beaumont Quay, 23, **31**, **32**, 32–3
Beccles, Suffolk, 153–4
Bell, Henry, 184, 185
Benham, Hervey, *Dawn Tops'l*, 67
Berney Hill, Norfolk, **146–7**
Blackshore, Suffolk, 133–5
Blackwell, Cy., 67
Blakeney, Norfolk, 166–7, **168**
Blakeney Point, 168–9
Bloom, Frank, 17, 22, 27
Blyford Bridge, Suffolk, 138–9
Blyth, river, 130–43

Blythburgh, Suffolk, 131, 136–8
Boulge, Suffolk, 95
Bowes-Vere Broke, Sir Philip, 79
Box, river, 60
Boxted Bridge, Suffolk, 61
Boyton, Suffolk, 114–15
Bradfield, Essex, 50
Bramble Island, Essex, 17, 30
Bramerton, Norfolk, 146, **149**
Bramerton Woods End, 146
Brancaster, Norfolk, 177
Brancaster Staithe, 175, **176**
Brantham, Suffolk, 55, **56**, 61, 62
Breydon Water, 145, 153, 158
Brinkley family, 88
Britten, Benjamin, 118, 124, 125, 127
  Peter Grimes, 128
Broke Hall, Suffolk, 79
Bromeswell, Suffolk, 101
Brundall, Norfolk, 146, **150**
Buckley, John, 134–5, 136
Bungay, Suffolk, 154–5
Bure, river, 145, 153
Bure Marshes National Nature Reserves, 151
Burgh Castle, Norfolk, 145
Burnham Deepdale, Norfolk, 175
Burnham Market, 174
Burnham Norton, 175
Burnham Overy, 174
Burnham Overy Staithe, 174, **175**
Burnham Thorpe, 174
Buss Creek, Suffolk, 135
Butley, river, 112, 114–15, **117**

Butley Ferry, Suffolk, 115
Butley Mills, 115–16
Butterman's Bay, Suffolk, 73

Canham, Kitty, 33–6
Catchpole, Margaret, 78–9, 109
Cattawade, Essex, 55
Cattawade Barrage, **54**, 55
Chelmondiston, Suffolk, 70
Chillesford, Suffolk, 116
Clarke, J.M., 76
Cley-next-the-Sea, Norfolk, 166, **167**
coastal erosion, 24–5, 127, 131
Cobbold, Revd Richard, 78
Cockshot Broad, 151
Collimer Point, Suffolk, 70
Collins, George, 102
Colne, river, 30, 34
Constable, Golding, 56
Constable, John, 14, 37, 57–8, 61, 62
Cooper, Winifred, 43, 44
Coots, Jack, H., 15
Copperas Bay, 48
Crabbe, George, 127–8, 154
Crozier, Eric, 125
Cumberland, Duke of, 141

Dalmeny, Lord, 34–6
Davidson, Revd Harold, 172
Deane, Anthony, 39
Deben, river, 86–105
Dedham, Suffolk, 57, 58–9
Defoe, Daniel, *Tour Through the Eastern Counties*, 96–7, 183
Denver, Norfolk, 188, 189–90
Dovercourt, Essex, 47, **49**
Doveys, Suffolk, 109
Downham Market, Norfolk, 189
Dowsing, William, 98, 137
Dunwich, Suffolk, 131, 137

Earsham Otter Trust, 155–6
East Bergholt, Suffolk, 57, 62
Edwards, Russell, *The River Stour*, 54
Elliott, John, 161
Erwarton Ness, Suffolk, 65–6

Fagbury Point, Suffolk, 81, 83–5
Falkenham, Suffolk, 88
Felixstowe, 12, 13, 81–3, 111
Felixstowe Ferry, 86, 87–8, *88–90*
Fingringhoe Wick Nature Reserve, Essex, 30
Fitzgerald, Edward, 95
Flatford, Suffolk, 37, 56–7

Friese Green, William, 45
Freston Park, Suffolk, 74
Freston Tower, 74, **75**

Gainsborough, Thomas, 14
Ganges, HMS, 11, 66, 67
Garrett, Newson, 124
Gedgrave, Suffolk, 107, 112
Gedgrave Cliff, 116–17
Geldeston Lock, Suffolk, 155
Goseford Haven, Suffolk, 88
Gough, Revd Henry, 34–6
Great Eastern Railway Company, 42
Great Ouse, 180, 188–90
Griffiths, Maurice, *The Magic of the Swatchways*, 19–21
Grimstone, Sir Harbottle, 50
Gull, Sir William Withey, 33

Halesworth–Southwold railway, 134, 142
Hamilton, Lady Emma, 45
Hamford Water, Essex, 17, 18, 21, 25, 29
Harkstead, Suffolk, 65
Harwich, Essex, 12, 13, 37–47, **48**
Havergate Island, Suffolk, 106–11, 119
Hawkes, Lt Col., 31
Heigham Sound, Norfolk, 152
Hemley, Suffolk, 89–90
Hickling Broad, 145, 151–2
Higham, Suffolk, 60
Holbrook, Suffolk, 63
Holbrook Bay, 63
Holbrook Creek, 50, 63, 67
Holbrook Royal Hospital School, 63
Holkham Bay, 173
Holkham Hall, 173
Holkham National Nature Reserve, 173–4
Hollesley, Suffolk, 113
Holme-next-the-Sea, Norfolk, 178
Holst, Imogen, 125, 127
Hopkins, Matthew, 53–4
Horsey Island, 17, 22, 29–30
Howard, Lady Katherine, 61
Hunstanton, 14, 178, 180

Iken, Suffolk, **122–3**, 123–4
International Boatbuilding Training Centre, Norfolk, 161–2
Ipswich, 75–8

James, M.R., 173
Jaques Bay, Essex, 50
Jones, Capt. Christopher, 37–8, 45

King's Fleet, Suffolk, 88
King's Lynn, Norfolk, 180, 183–8
Kirton marshes, Suffolk, 89
Kirby Creek, Essex, 17, 30
Kirby-le-Soken, Essex, 23, 28
Kyson Point, Suffolk, 92, **93**

Lake Lothing, Suffolk, 158, 161–2
Landermere, Essex, 31–2, 33, **34**
Landermere Creek, 17, 19, 23, **29**
Langham, Essex, 59–60
Langham, Norfolk, 171–2
Laud, Will, 78–9, 109
Levington Creek, Suffolk, 79–80
lightships, 40–1
Little Oakley, Essex, 22, 23
Lowe, Richard, 176–7
Lowestoft, Suffolk, 158, 162
Luff, John, 78–9, 108

Malster, Robert,
   Ipswich – Town on the Orwell, 78
   Wherries & Waterways, 157, 161
Malthouse Broad, 151
malting trade, 51, 124–5
Maltings, Snape, 124–5
Manningtree, Essex, 47, 51, 53–4, 61
Marine Aircraft Experimental Establishment, Parkeston Quay, 12, 83
Martello Towers, 43–4, 87, 113, 128
Martlesham, Suffolk, 92
Mayer, Dr Sue, 182–3
Mayflower, 37, 38, 45
Melton, 99
   Old Melton Church, 100
Minsmere, Suffolk, 108, 132
Mistley, Essex, 51–3, 67
Moore, Derek, 85
Morston, Norfolk, 169, 171
Munnings, Sir Alfred, 59

Nacton, Suffolk, 78–9
Nayland, Suffolk, 61
Naze cliffs, Essex, 23–6
Nelson, Lord Horatio, 37, 45, 154, 174
Newbourn, Suffolk, 90
Norfolk Coast Path, 178
Norfolk Broads, 144–64
Norfolk keels, 157
Norfolk Wherry Trust, 158–61

Oakley Creek, Essex, 17, 29–30
Ore, river, 107–14
Orford, Suffolk, 106, 107, 108, 117–19, 120

Orfordness, 120–2
Orwell, river, 68–85
Orwell Bridge, Suffolk, 75
Orwell Park, Suffolk, 79
Ostrich Creek, Suffolk, 75, 77
otters, 155–6
Oulton Broad, 153, 158

Parkeston Quay, Essex, 13, 38, **41**, 42
Partis, Bob, 64
Partridge, John, 106, 110, 111
Partridge, Reg, 111
Pears, Peter, 124, 125, 127
Peddars Way, 178
Peewit Island, Essex, 17, 30
Pepys, Samuel, 37, 39
Perryman, John, 159, 161
Pin Mill, Suffolk, 11, 70–3
Piper, John, 127
Puffin (launch), 63–4, **65**

Quilter family, 87–8

Raedwald, Saxon king, 98
Ramsey, Essex, 47
Ramsholt, Suffolk, 102–3
Ransome, Arthur, *Secret Water*, 21
Ranworth Broad, 150–1
Reed, Joe, 168, 169
Reedham, Norfolk, 157, 158
Reedham Ferry, 156–7
Rendlesham Forest, Suffolk, 102
Rennie, John, 189
Reydon, Suffolk, 135, **136**, 139
Rigby, Richard, 52
Roberts, Bob, *The Last of the Sailormen*, 72
   A Slice of Suffolk, 72
RSPB reserves, 48, 106–11, 165, 178

Salthouse, Norfolk, 166
Sandlings, Suffolk, 101–2
Saxons, 68, 97–8
Scolt Head Island, Norfolk, 175–7
Seal Assessment Centre, Docking, 169, 182–3
seals, 18, 119, 169–71, 181–3
Sea Mammal Research Unit, Cambridge, 181–2
Seckford, Thomas, 94
Shingle Street, Suffolk, 112–13
Shotley, Suffolk, 38, 62, 70
Shotley Gate, 66
Shotley Point, 38, 66–7, 68, 69
Sizewell, Suffolk, 13, 132

Skippers Island, Essex, 17, 22, **27**, **28**, 30–1
Slaughden, Suffolk, 112, **125**, 127–9
Sleighton Hill, Suffolk, 81
smuggling, 70, 73, 135
Snape, Suffolk, 124–6
Snape Maltings, 124–5
Snape Warren, 126
snowgeese, 129
Snow Goose, The (film), 29
Sole Bay, battle of (1672), 141–2
Southwold, Suffolk, 131, 133–4, 140–3
'stackies', **30**, 32–3, 66
Stiffkey, Norfolk, 172
Stoke-by-Nayland, Suffolk, 37, 61
Stone Point, Essex, 25
Stour Estuary, 37–55, 66–7
Stour Valley, 14, 55–65
Stour Wood, 48
Stratford St Mary, Suffolk, 59
Stutton, Suffolk, 62
Stutton Ness, 63
Sudbury, Suffolk, 14, 55
Surlingham, Norfolk, 146
Sutton Hoo, Suffolk, 97–8, 101

Tennyson, Julian, *Suffolk Scene*, 123
Thorington Mill, Suffolk, 60
Thorington Street, 60
Thorpe-le-Soken, Essex, 28, 33, **35**, 36
Thurne, river, 145, 151
Titchwell, Norfolk, 178
Tomline, Col. George, 79
Trimley Marshes, Suffolk, 81, 84–5
Trimley St Martin & St Mary, 81
Trinity House, 40–1, 121
Tunstall Forest, Suffolk, 102

Ufford, Suffolk, 98
Underwood, Charles, 121

Vernon, Admiral, 79
Viking invasions, 68

Wade, river, 17
Walberswick, Suffolk, 130–2
Waldringfield, Suffolk, 90–1, **92**
Walton Backwaters, 17–36
Walton-on-the-Naze, Essex, 21, **23**, **24**, 26–8
Waveney, river, 145, 155
Wayre, Philip & Jeane, 155
Wells-next-the-Sea, Norfolk, 172–3
Wenhaston, Suffolk, 139
West Norfolk Seal Rescue, King's Lynn, 183
wherries, 157–61
Wiggenhall St German, Norfolk, 189
Wiggenhall St Mary Magdalen, 189
Wiggenhall St Mary the Virgin, 189
Wiggenhall St Peter, 189
Wilford Bridge, Suffolk, 99, 101
witchcraft, evidence of, 54
witch-hunting, 53–4
Wolsey Creek, Suffolk, 136, 139
Woodbridge, Suffolk, 92–7
wool and cloth trade, 53, 59, 61, 118, 137
Woolverstone Park, Suffolk, 73–4
World War I, 141
Wrabness, Essex, 48–9, 67
Wroxham, 148, 152–3

Yare, river, 145, 146, 156
Yarmouth, 162–4